The Caring Elder

A Training Manual for Serving

Victor A. Constien

CONCORDIA PUBLISHING HOUSE · SAINT LOUIS

Biblical references are from the Revised Standard Version of the Bible, copyrighted 1946, 1952, © 1971, 1973. Used by permission.

Copyright © 1986 by Concordia Publishing House, 3558 S. Jefferson Ave., St. Louis, MO 63118-3968. Manufactured in the United States of America.

Library of Congress Cataloging-in-Publication Data

Constien, Victor A., 1929-
  The caring elder.

  1. Elders (Church officers) I. Title.
BV680.C66 1986   253   85-26507
ISBN 0-570-03993-2

14 15   05

Contents

	Page
For Your Reading . . . and Much More	4
1. Why Elders?	5
2. The Congregation's Expectations	13
3. Who Are These Elders?	21
4. Elders Assist in Congregational Worship	28
5. Elders Help Others Learn and Teach the Gospel of Christ, Too	37
6. Elders Promote Witnessing to Christ, the World's Savior	46
7. Elders Equip Servants of Jesus, the Compassionate Lord	54
8. Elders Build Up Congregational Fellowship and Support	62
9. Evaluating Elders	73
Appendix A – 200 Bible Readings for an Elder's Personal Devotions	81
Appendix B – An Elder's Prayers	87
Appendix C – Personal Pages for an Elder's Goals, Diary, and Records	89
Appendix D – Six Devotions for Elders Meetings	92
Appendix E – Five Bible Studies for Elders Meetings	105

For Your Reading . . . and Much More

This book is for you to read, of course. Whether you are an elder in your congregation, a member of an elders zone, a called church worker, or chairman of a nominating committee, personally scanning these pages will increase your appreciation for an elder's service to Christ Jesus and a congregation of His people.

You should also be stimulated by your reading to include the work of elders in your prayers. More aware of the extensive and sensitive areas in which elders minister with other Christians, you will perceive the need for God's blessing. Only through total dependence on Jesus will elders be able to carry out their divinely given tasks.

As a guide for discussion the book can become a valuable tool for elders' growth. Those who recently have been elected as elders can use the book in orienting themselves to their new calling. A preservice training manual you might call it.

In another setting, a congregation with a seasoned board of elders can use this book to review and evaluate the elder's position description and the strengths and weaknesses of the board's current operation. As effective as board members are, by God's grace they are always in the process of becoming even better representatives of His mercy in Christ Jesus.

Debating answers to the questions at the end of each session will lead you to reflect more deeply on the role of the elder in a Christian congregation. Discussion in elders meetings and training events can also provoke you to some exciting decisions about new hopes, goals, and strategies for your congregation in the mission of Jesus Christ.

1.
Why Elders?

Todd James and his wife Emelda were stumped. Seated at their kitchen table, they were trying to complete a questionnaire. Their congregation's officers wanted feedback on parish programs.

One set of questions focused on the elders as spiritual leaders.

"I thought our pastor was our spiritual leader," Emelda said. "He's been trained for it. God called him to his vocation, and our congregation called him to this location."

Todd agreed. "I wonder whether ordinary people like elders or the rest of us members in the congregation can ever really guide someone else's spiritual life. Isn't that the pastor's job?" he asked.

Members of Lutheran congregations like Mr. and Mrs. James may assume that elders simply come with the package. Join the congregation and you get a board of elders with it. You may even be assigned to an elder. You may not be sure why, but if that's the system, it probably won't hurt you.

Some elders themselves may not have probed very deeply the reasons for their eldership, the rationale for their position. Parish constitutions and bylaws sometimes do little more than state briefly the elders' duties. Orientation or training sessions for elders may be superficial, if conducted at all. However, the elders of a congregation need and deserve more than a handshake to welcome them to their jobs.

It becomes clear that the elders we read about in the Old and New Testaments did not serve the same role as elders in our congregations today. However, we can learn from those early spiritual guides something about leadership among God's people in every age, including our own.

So the goals of this first session are that you (1) discover differences in the ways Biblical authors wrote about elders and the meanings we attach to the word "elder" today, (2) identify leadership qualifications among Old and New Testament elders which congregation officers might imitate today, and (3) list at least two reasons why a contemporary congregation appoints people to the position of elder.

Elders in the Old Testament

In Old Testament times elders served God's people. In Exodus 3 we note that God chose Moses to lead the people of Israel out of slavery in Egypt. But Moses was uncertain about his credibility. He asked God what he should tell Israel about the name of the God of their fathers who sent him. God said to Moses, "I AM WHO I AM . . . Say this to the people of Israel, 'I AM has sent me to you.'" God also explained to Moses that His name is "The Lord, the God of your fathers, the God of Abraham, the God of Isaac, and the God of Jacob . . . My name forever, and thus I am to be remembered throughout all generations."

God further instructed Moses, "Go and gather the elders of Israel together, and say to them, 'The Lord, the God of your fathers, the God of Abraham, of Isaac, and of Jacob, has appeared to me, saying, "I have observed you and what has been done to you in Egypt; and I promise that I will bring you up out of the affliction of Egypt, to the land of the Canaanites, the Hittites, the Amorites, the Perizzites, the Hivites, and the Jebusites, a land flowing with milk and honey."'"

God promised Moses that the people would listen to him. Then God continued, "And you and the elders of Israel shall go to the king of Egypt and say to him, 'The Lord, the God of the Hebrews, has met with us; and now, we pray you, let us go a three days' journey into the wilderness, that we may sacrifice to the Lord our God.' I know that the king of Egypt will not let you go unless compelled by a mighty hand. So I will stretch out My hand and smite Egypt with all the wonders I will do in it; after that he will let you go."

Although no writer in the Old Testament tells how elders were appointed, they obviously played significant leadership roles. They obeyed powerful figures like Moses and Joshua, while at the same time they acted for the whole people of Israel at major events. Perhaps at one time the elders were heads of families or clans. Later they represented the entire nation.

Elders directed the Passover celebration (Exodus 12:21-27). They came with Aaron to eat bread with Jethro, Moses' father-in-law, as he offered burnt offerings and sacrifices to God (Exodus 18:12). In the sight of the elders Moses struck the rock at Horeb from which God miraculously poured out water for His people to drink (Exodus 17:6). The elders of Israel joined Joshua for the attack on Ai (Joshua 8:10).

When God heard the people of Israel complaining about their misfortunes in the wilderness, He said to Moses, "Gather for Me seventy men of the elders of Israel, whom you know to be the elders of the people and officers over them; and bring them to the tent of the meeting, and let them take their stand there with you. And I will come down and talk with you there; and I will take some of the spirit which is upon you and put it on them; and they shall bear the burden of the people with you that you may not bear it yourself alone" (Numbers 11:16-17). Moses then appointed special elders to share his leadership burdens.

At Mount Sinai God invited 70 elders to come up to Him with Aaron, Nadab, and Abihu and worship afar off. Only Moses came near to the Lord. But the elders of Israel were there, too. "And they saw the God of Israel; and there was under His feet as it were a pavement of sapphire stone, like the very heaven for clearness. And He did not lay His hand on the chief men of the people of Israel; they beheld God, and ate and drank" (Exodus 24:10-11).

Later when Israel received a king, the elders lost some of their influence. Nevertheless, in a time of crisis, such as described in 1 Kings 20, kings like Ahab wisely called in all the elders of the land for advice. Kings coveted and needed the support of the elders.

At the time of Jesus' birth, the ruling body of the Jews was called the Sanhedrin. Also known as the Council of Elders, it eventually became the high court, the chief authority for interpreting the Law and instructing the scribes.

Elders in the New Testament

We first read about elders in the Christian church in Jerusalem in Acts 11. Luke wrote that Agabus forecast a great famine all over the world. When it came, "the disciples determined, everyone according to his ability, to send relief to the brethren who lived in Judea; and they did so, sending it to the elders by the hand of Barnabas and Saul" (vv. 29-30).

Later a dispute arose over the question "Can a person be saved without circumcision?" At the height of the discussion, "Paul and Barnabas and some of the others were appointed to go up to Jerusalem to the apostles and the elders about this question. . . . When they came to Jerusalem, they were welcomed by the church and the apostles and the elders, and they declared all that God had done with them" (Acts 15:2-4).

Following the apostolic council, as Paul and Timothy "went on their way through the cities, they delivered to them for observances the decisions which had been reached by the apostles and elders who were at Jerusalem. So the churches were strengthened in the faith, and they increased in numbers daily" (Acts 16:4-5).

In Acts 21:17-20a, Luke reported: "When we had come to Jerusalem, the brethren received us gladly. On the following day, Paul went in with us to James; and all the elders were present. After greeting them, he related one by one the things that God had done among the Gentiles through his ministry. And when they heard it they glorified God." Representing the Jerusalem congregation, the elders assembled for their meetings under the chairmanship of the apostle James. As mature and experienced members they helped to monitor with the apostles the teaching of the Gospel of Christ throughout the church.

When Paul and Barnabas evangelized communities and organized clusters of believers, they appointed elders and with prayer and fasting committed them to the Lord in whom they believed (Acts 14:23). After the apostles left to continue their work in other places, these elders built on the foundations the apostles had laid.

In his farewell speech to the elders from Ephesus (Acts 20:17-38), Paul shared the whole counsel of God. He named the elders guardians of God's people who were to "care for the church of God which He obtained with the blood of His own Son." He urged them to be alert for fierce wolves who attack the flock from without and perverse men from within who try to draw away Christians after them. Appointed by the apostles, the elders preserved the teaching of the apostles, and trained and guided the company of believers.

Perhaps writing from Rome, the apostle Peter also drafted instructions for congregations in Asia Minor. "So I exhort the elders among you, as a fellow elder and a witness of the sufferings of Christ as well as a partaker in the glory that is to be revealed. Tend the flock of God that is your charge, not by constraint but willingly, not for shameful gain but eagerly, not as domineering over those in your charge but being examples to the flock" (1 Peter 5:1-3). Obviously, these elders had authority. But they were to be models for believers, responsible to Jesus, the Chief Shepherd, who comes on the Day of Fulfillment to give the "unfading crown of glory" to those who in faith wait for His appearing.

The apostle Paul urged the young minister Timothy to recall the action of the elders at his ordination. "Do not neglect the gift you have, which was given you by prophetic utterance when the council of elders laid their hands upon you," Paul wrote. ". . . Take heed to yourself and to your teaching; hold to that, for by so doing you will save both yourself and your hearers" (1 Timothy 4:14, 16). The word Paul used here reveals the tradition of a "college of elders" at the time.

When he wrote to Titus, another young pastor, the apostle Paul requested elders for the sake of good order. "This is why I left you in Crete," Paul penned, "that you might amend what was defective, and appoint elders in every town as I directed you, if any man is blameless, the husband of one wife and his children are believers and not open to the charge of being profligate or insubordinate" (Titus 1:5-6).

Paul encouraged Christians to recognize the faithful service of elders. "Let the elders who rule well be considered worthy of double honor, especially those who labor in preaching and teaching," Paul taught Timothy (1 Timothy 5:17). Paul also wanted the elders to be protected in their work. "Never admit any charge against an elder except on the evidence of two or three witnesses," he wrote (1 Timothy 5:19).

The apostle John called himself "the elder" when he wrote the opening verses of his second and third letters. By this term he probably did not mean that he spoke as an elected official. Rather, he was a highly respected teacher, a spiritual person who cherished and shared the teachings of Jesus.

The 24 elders described in the Book of Revelation are seated around the throne of God. They perform no ruling function. Instead, they revel in the majesty of God as they "fall down before Him who is seated on the throne and worship Him who lives forever and ever; they cast their crowns before the throne, singing, 'Worthy art Thou, our Lord and God, to receive glory and honor and power, for Thou didst create all things, and by Thy will they existed and were created' " (Revelation 4:10-11).

Deacons in the New Testament

Like elders, deacons are also identified in the New Testament as close associates with pastors, or bishops. In the opening verses of his Letter to the Philippians, Paul with Timothy conveyed grace and peace from God our Father and the Lord Jesus Christ "to all the saints in Christ Jesus who are at Philippi, with the bishops and deacons."

Immediately after detailing the qualifications of a bishop in his First Letter to Timothy, Paul wrote, "Deacons likewise must be serious, not double-tongued, not addicted to much wine, not greedy for gain; they must hold the mystery of the faith with a clear conscience" (1 Timothy 3:8-9).

Deacons dedicated themselves to serving others in personally helpful ways. They demonstrated the meaning of their name by being "servants" or "table waiters." While in the New Testament we see no clear distinction between elders and deacons, authors who wrote later mention bishops, elders, and deacons as three separate groups.

Required by God?

Because we read so much about elders in the Bible we naturally ask, "Does God command congregations to appoint elders? Is the office of elder divinely mandated?"

Our search of the Scriptures yielded only one answer, "No." At no time in His relationship with His people has God said that congregations of believers must have a college or board of elders. People called elders have served God's people through the centuries. They have helped over the years to guide the spiritual development of brothers and sisters in the faith. But God never has said that congregations must appoint such a group of officers.

When we ask the same question about pastors, we receive a different answer. The office of the public ministry, as carried out by the pastor of a congregation, is God's way of exercising the Office of the Keys. God requires congregations to have pastors. The Scriptures mandate the office of the public ministry. The apostle Paul told the Christians at Ephesus that the gifts of God Himself "were that some should be apostles, some prophets, some evangelists, some pastors and teachers, to equip the saints for the work of ministry" (Ephesians 4:11-12).

In 1 Timothy 3:2 ff. and Titus 1:5 ff. Paul described the kind of bishop, or pastor, which God requires for His people: men who are above reproach, blameless, the husband of one wife, not arrogant or quick-tempered, sensible, dignified, an apt teacher, hospitable, not violent or greedy for gain or a drunkard, a lover of goodness, upright, holy, and self-controlled.

In his office as bishop, or pastor, Timothy received counsel from Paul to command and teach pure doctrine, attend to the public reading and preaching of the Scriptures, oversee the spiritual lives of people, and encourage Christians to pray for all people. Obviously, Timothy was not to do all this simply out of his own tool box of ideas but according to the plans and power God provided through Paul's instructions.

The writer of the Letter to the Hebrews charged early Christians to value the pastors who as God's representatives spoke His Word: "Obey your leaders and submit to them; for they are keeping watch over your souls, as men who will have to give account. Let them do this joyfully, and not sadly, for that would be of no advantage to you" (Hebrews 13:17).

Close Relationships with the Pastor

Obviously, a congregation which by divine mandate calls a pastor for the public ministry, and by the instruction of its constitution and bylaws appoints a board of elders to assist the pastor, wants its pastor and elders to work in harmony. We know that God intends a close working relationship because of the language of the apostle Paul in his First Letter to Timothy.

Paul said, "Do not rebuke an older man but exhort him as you would a father; treat younger men like brothers, older women like mothers, younger women like sisters, in all purity" (5:1). A pastor is to treat the people of his flock as members of one family. It stands to reason the members and the board of elders as their representatives also have close ties to their pastor.

Members of a congregation's board of elders are not assistant pastors. They *assist* their pastor. They are not officially called to perform the Office of the Keys. They work closely with the pastor, who is called to perform this office. We might say that elders are assistants to the pastor. They help generate excitement and support for the preaching and teaching of the Word of God.

A congregation may call more than one person to serve on the team which carries out the office of the public ministry. The elders' task in such a congregation becomes even more vital. Through the senior pastor, elders establish a caring link with each person on the professional staff, whether assistant pastor; director of Christian education, evangelism, youth, or music; principal or faculty member of the parish elementary school; deaconess; or parish assistant. But, even more important, elders help facilitate and strengthen the working relationships of the church staff. Their experience and loving concern provide a creative context in which to review staff structure, operations, and climate. Meetings of a team of church workers can always be improved as can the team's interaction with other people who are partners in the Gospel. Elders work for those improvements.

Close Relationships with Other Boards

Because elders serve all the members of the congregation, seeking the total spiritual health of each person, elders need to remain in intimate contact with the members of the other committees and boards of the congregation. This contact can often best be maintained through the meetings of the coordinating or church council or board of directors.

Some elders may also play a prominent role in the parish planning council. Here they can evangelically influence the coordinated programs by which the congregation pursues its goals. If a congregation does not have a planning council, the board of elders might fulfill the planning function until a council is appointed.

Meeting at least three times during the summer months and once in December to plan, evaluate, and adjust parish goals and the programs to meet them, the planning council consists of representatives of all the congregation's major activities. In concert they help compose and play out the chief themes, aims, and strategies the congregation chooses for its ministry of the Word of God each year. However they do it, either by initiating a planning council or by taking the task to themselves, elders help the congregation set short-term and long-range goals and then marshal the resources to accomplish them.

Confronting the Challenge

The goals for this session, again, are that you (1) discover differences in the ways Biblical authors wrote about elders and the meanings we attach to the word "elder" today, (2) identify leadership qualifications among Old and New Testament elders which congregation officers might imitate today, and (3) list at least two reasons why a contemporary congregation appoints people to the position of elder.

As you work toward these goals, complete and discuss the items below.

1. Summarize why the people of Israel had elders.

_____

_____

2. Compare some of the reasons for elders revealed by New Testament authors with those indicated in the Old Testament.

_____

_____

3. Describe at least three leadership qualifications among Biblical elders which elders in your congregation might imitate.

_____

_____

4. Examine the constitution and bylaws of your congregation. Look carefully for references to elders. Compare the qualifications for elders in these documents with those you observed in reading the Biblical pas-

sages. Note similarities and differences.

_____

_____

5. From your congregation's constitution and bylaws or from your discussion of the work of elders in this session, write two reasons why your congregation appoints elders.

_____

_____

6. Why did you accept your appointment as an elder? What doubts, convictions, or joys accompany your decision?

_____

_____

7. A. How would you evaluate the working relationship of your board of elders with the pastor and professional staff of your congregation?

Total Disaster	**Barely Tolerable**	**Organized but Average**	**Fairly Exciting**	**Altogether Perfect**

B. Suggest one step to improve this relationship.

_____

_____

8. A. How would you evaluate the working relationship of your board of elders with the other boards and committees of the congregation?

Total Disaster	**Barely Tolerable**	**Organized but Average**	**Fairly Exciting**	**Altogether Perfect**

B. Suggest one step to improve this relationship.

_____

_____

9. List at least two printed resources or training events you intend to use this coming year to help you grasp more fully the reasons why your congregation appoints elders and to help you work more effectively with your pastor and church staff and other boards and committees.

_____

_____

2.
The Congregation's Expectations

Joe Abscott was not altogether surprised by the phone call. He had heard a rumor that the nominating committee considered him a potential candidate for a church office. So when his friend Phil Brandon called from the committee meeting, he did not hang up on Phil.

However, Joe was shaken up a little when he heard Phil say, "We want to nominate you for the board of elders. It's one of the most important jobs in the congregation. Will you accept?"

Although Joe had been a member of the congregation for six years, he had not yet served on any official committee. He faithfully attended worship services, the Lord's Supper, and the adult Sunday Bible class but was not involved in what he called the "business structure" of the parish.

Joe knew that before he could answer Phil's question he must do some homework. He needed to know what the congregation expected of its elders. Then after praying about the opportunity and discussing it with some other members of the congregation, he would be better prepared to reply to the invitation. And Phil wanted an answer by next Thursday!

Goals

The goals of this session zero in on the parish expectations about which Joe speculated. As you work through the next few pages you will identify goals and functions for your congregation's board of elders. You will also describe the elder's role in Christian discipline and restoration in the congregation, discuss the organization of the board of elders for service in elders zones, and agree on an agenda for conducting elders meetings.

What's a Board of Elders to Do?

Normally, we look to the constitution and bylaws for a clear statement of what the congregation expects its board of elders to do.

For example, your congregation may call its board of elders the department of worship and spiritual life, consisting of one elder for each zone into which the congregation divides itself, plus one elder who serves as chairman. He administers no zone.

If the term of office for each elder is three years, one-third of the board's membership is selected each year.

The chairman usually represents the board at meetings of the church council, or the coordinating council.

Your congregation will expect its elders to assist the pastor in all matters pertaining to the spiritual welfare of the congregation. It may charge the elders "to assist the pastor with the supervision of public worship and church discipline." Additional bylaws should explain the implications of the charge.

Your congregation may want its elders to emphasize Matthew 28:19, the command of our Lord Jesus to "go and make disciples of all people." The elders will then exercise special care for the people in their zone, encouraging growth in faith toward God and love toward each neighbor.

Elders should be concerned about their own spiritual growth and avail themselves of the opportunities for periodic training.

So that no parish member is ignored or abandoned, elders should assist the church office in keeping an accurate membership file, accounting for each person who enters or leaves the congregation. Prompt transfers of members moving in and out demonstrate Christian care.

Specific Functions

When congregations describe in more detail the functions of their board of elders, they may say something like this:

1. "Pray for, encourage, and be concerned about the spiritual, emotional, and physical health and welfare of the pastor and his family (adequate compensation, housing, free time, vacation, assistance in times of illness), and to that end specifically review these items once a year."

2. "Counsel with the pastor so that the Word of God is preached in truth and purity, the holy sacraments are administered in accordance with Christ's institution, and Lutheran doctrine and practices are preserved in the congregation."

3. "Assist the pastor in counseling with difficult cases and in finding peaceful and God-pleasing solutions to spiritual problems within the congregation."

4. "Encourage spiritual growth through regular church attendance, study of the Word, frequent reception of the Lord's Supper, a more active prayer life, and increased involvement in the mission of the church."

5. "Direct and supervise the visitation of all members and make every effort to enlist them in the work of the church."

6. "Make a strong effort to get to know every member of the elder group, to try to become aware of temporal needs, sickness and death in the family, and other special situations in which the congregation can be of help, both in prayer and in other action."

7. "Determine eligibility for membership of all individuals and families applying for membership in the congregation, according to

Article _____ of the Constitution and Article _____ of the Bylaws."

8. "Exercise discipline within the congregation according to Scripture, the Lutheran Confessions, and Article _____ of the Bylaws, and insure that the congregation functions in accordance with the established doctrine of the church as listed in Article _____ of the Constitution."

9. "Help maintain a proper relationship with The Lutheran Church—Missouri Synod in order adequately to support Christ's mission throughout the world."

10. "Engage in member conservation. Review Communion and church attendance of all members. Make calls on delinquents and follow up on all newborn children in the congregation until they are baptized."

11. "Supervise the thorough instruction of children, youth, and adults for Baptism, first Communion, the rite of confirmation, and the rite of reaffirmation of faith for membership in the congregation."

12. "Be responsible for a friendly, personal welcome of visitors at worship and for reception, orientation, and integration of new members in conjunction with the Board of Evangelism."

13. "Assist and advise, in consultation with the pastor, all established auxiliary organizations. Encourage spiritual programs in the societies of the congregation generally."

14. "Participate in the training events the pastor conducts for elders according to a schedule upon which the pastor and elders mutually agree."

15. "When the pastor permanently moves to another assignment, make arrangements for interim pastoral services until the new pastor arrives."

16. "Submit an annual budget request in the form and at the time requested by the congregation's department of stewardship."

Subcommittees

A board of elders may decide to divide itself into subcommittees. Such subcommittees bring recommendations to the entire board for approval. Only the board itself can make decisions on matters entrusted to it by the congregation. But a subcommittee may facilitate board action and thus improve board services with the members of the parish.

Subcommittees may work on such tasks as worship, membership orientation, or membership conservation. Sometimes a board may assign the implementation of one of its programs or parts thereof to a subcommittee, but the board is always accountable for this implementation to the congregation.

A worship subcommittee, for example, might assist the board of elders in the following ways:

1. Provide well-administered, orderly worship services. Plan and publicize the services for the year.

2. Approve and disapprove new forms of worship, liturgies, and hymns for use in public worship.

3. Supervise and provide for the ministry of music for the worship services and other functions. Annually appoint a director of music. Supervise the music for all services and cooperate with the organist, the choir director, and choir members in maintaining high musical standards for the service of worship. Annually review compensation.

4. Together with the pastor set the time, schedule, and number of Communion services. Assist the pastor with Communion distribution, reading the Scripture, preaching, etc., as required.

5. Maintain an adequate supply of expendable items for worship, such as Communion cards, pencils, Communion wine and wafers, baptismal napkins, candles, etc., in conjunction with the altar guild.

6. Supervise the altar guild in the care, use, and maintenance of the sacred vessels, the altar, the altar furnishings, vestments, and all chancel decorations, and the distribution of altar flowers to people who are sick and shut-in.

7. Supervise the recruitment, training, and services of the ushers.

8. Maintain and supervise adequate facilities and personnel for the nursery to care for children during worship services and adult Bible classes.

Subcommittees responsible for other tasks of the elders would, of course, be instructed by a different set of guidelines.

Christian Discipline and Restoration

Perhaps Joe Abscott hesitated to accept his friend Phil's nomination to the board of elders because he had been led to believe that the board's most challenging job is "church discipline."

"The steps to excommunication are involved here," Joe mused to himself. "I don't know whether I want to get that involved in a person's life. Other people are better qualified for that than I am. On the other hand, it does sound like important church work."

If Joe eventually serves on the board of elders he will happily discover that the purpose of Christian discipline is restoration, not exclusion. He will also be confirmed in his conviction that elders involved in Christian discipline do indeed engage in a vital ministry. They imitate the apostle Paul who instructed the Christians in Corinth to remove from their fellowship the man who lived immorally with his father's wife. However, Paul issued his judgment in the name of Jesus against the sinner in order "that his spirit may be saved in the day of the Lord Jesus" (1 Corinthians 5:5). That's always the reason for church discipline. God has not designed His program of care in order to annihilate people but to rescue them. He commissioned His Son, Jesus, to save people, not destroy them.

Another reason for Christian discipline is to wake us all up to the seriousness of unrepented sin. Paul charged the young pastor Timothy, "As for those who persist in sin, rebuke them in the presence of all, so that the rest may stand in fear" (1 Timothy 5:20). As we are moved by God's Spirit to fear sin and its consequences, we are assured by the same

Spirit that when we confess our sins, God is faithful and just to pardon us.

For whom does a board of elders show special concern? Who receives Christian discipline? We noted already from Paul's Letter to the Corinthians that persistent, blatant, immoral behavior puts a person in spiritual jeopardy. Unless the guilty person repents, God's final judgment falls and the person is eternally lost. People who continue in open, defiant sin are the primary target for Christian discipline—that they may repent and be saved.

Paul also called for the exercise of Christian discipline against people who teach contrary to the Gospel of Christ. When Judaizers tempted the Christians in Galatia to return to a salvation by Law apart from faith in Christ, Paul wrote, "As we have said before, so now I say again, if anyone is preaching to you a gospel contrary to that which you received, let him be accursed" (Galatians 1:9). Because false teachers are not always easily discerned, the board of elders needs to equip itself with full knowledge of the chief teachings of the Scriptures and the Lutheran Confessions. Only as elders are immersed in Christian doctrine can they begin to measure the teaching of someone else.

How are elders to administer Christian discipline? First, they prepare themselves. "With the judgment you pronounce you will be judged," Jesus told His followers, "and the measure you give will be the measure you get. Why do you see the speck that is in your brother's eye, but do not notice the log that is in your own eye? . . . You hypocrite, first take the log out of your own eye, and then you will see clearly to take the speck out of your brother's eye" (Matthew 7:2-5). Elders who in a repentant spirit trust God's personal forgiveness in Christ can then help others seek and trust that forgiveness for themselves. As elders first test themselves against God's law, admitting their sins against Him and pleading for His pardon, they become fitted by God's Spirit to participate in the Christian discipline of erring brothers and sisters in the faith. Since God is the final judge, all Christian discipline by members of Christ's church here on earth should be patient and loving without vindictive pride or arrogant superiority.

Jesus said that after personal preparation the first step in church discipline is, "If your brother sins against you, go and tell him his fault, between you and him alone. If he listens to you, you have gained your brother" (Matthew 18:15). Aware that a Christian has committed a serious sin but has not acknowledged it as disobedience toward God, a board of elders is to arrange for a fellow Christian, humbly and in private, to confront the person, identify the sin, and urge repentance. If the person refuses, elders may decide that this first step should be repeated, perhaps several times. While Jesus said that this step should be taken at least once, He did not limit the number of times it may be repeated. Patient persistence may convert the sinner from the error of his ways. Then joy breaks out in heaven and on earth.

However, a person may refuse to listen to the admonition, or deny any guilt, or reject the claim that the act was sinful, or continue in the sin even after making a promise to change. "But if he does not listen," Jesus said, "take one or two others along with you, that every word may be confirmed by the evidence of two or three witnesses" (Matthew 18:16). Some of the person's friends may be especially effective. At any rate, the two or three fellow Christians who assist should be mature and compassionate people in whom the confronted person may have confidence. Then if repentance results, the whole matter remains within the small circle of caring witnesses, and the person is restored to the joy of full partnership in the company of believers.

"If he refuses to listen to them, tell it to the church," Jesus concluded, "and if he refuses to listen even to the church, let him be to you as a Gentile and a tax collector. Truly, I say to you, whatever you bind on earth shall be bound in heaven, and whatever you loose on earth shall be loosed in heaven" (Matthew 18:17-18).

The next step, as Jesus instructs, is taken by the whole congregation. In their prayers and conversations they plead for and with the person who so far refuses to repent. The fellow Christians who have already talked privately with the person share information about their visits. They confirm that the person has sinned and that they have tried to persuade the offended to repent and to stop sinning, accepting God's forgiveness through faith in Christ. But the person has rejected their counsel. So the entire parish becomes convinced that the situation is serious. All the members are requested to minister lovingly with the person, attempting to effect a return to faith in God's pardon and active participation in the family of Christ.

The final act by which the Christian congregation tries to make the person aware of the gravity of the sin is excommunication. Yet, even as the offender is excluded from its fellowship, the congregation compassionately yearns for the repentance and return in faith of this person for whom Christ died. Plans are then made immediately by the evangelism board of the parish to continue a Christian witness to the person for whom the congregation desires salvation, not eternal death.

Elders Zones

Many congregations have discovered the benefits of organizing their members in elders zones. According to one set of bylaws "the Board of Elders shall be elected by the congregation through the Voters Assembly, one elder for each 20 communicant families, or major fraction thereof, in the congregation." Other congregations recognize elders groups consisting of numbers of members which vary from zone to zone. Some parishes divide their membership along geographic lines, clustering families who live close to one another in the same zone. Other congregations organize zones so that the members form a creative mix, enriching one another's lives out of their experience in different ethnic and cultural backgrounds.

The primary purpose of an elders zone is to enable the members of the congregation intentionally and more intimately to care for one another in Christian fellowship. Even in small congregations hectic personal life-styles sometimes prevent people from knowing the needs of neighbors or the resources they have to offer the larger community. In small groups Christians can more quickly learn to know one another. They can also more easily identify ways to bring healing to those who hurt, encouragement to those who despair, physical help to those who are sick, forgiveness to those who feel their guilt, and friendship to those who are lonely.

A congregation may ask people to aid an elder who administers a large zone. Assistants can help make regular visits in the homes with respect to congregational goals and performance. As the members of elders zones stimulate one another to regular attendance at worship, the Lord's Supper, and classes for the study of the Scriptures, they build up the entire congregation for its Christian mission. Some zones may choose to conduct "study and care" sessions which rotate among members' homes over a month or six times each year.

An Agenda for Elders Meetings

Obviously, an agenda for meetings of the board of elders in congregations with zones includes time for elders to share ideas on how to improve interaction among their sisters and brothers in Christ. Elders also need to develop new skills for listening to genuine concerns and providing appropriate Christian responses. That takes time and training, too.

How might elders fit other elements into their regular meetings? Here's a suggestion for a two-hour session.

1. Getting reacquainted: sharing personal concerns
2. Studying the Scriptures together
3. Praying for parish members, professional church workers, and fellow elders
4. Learning from needs and successes in the zones or from elders' visits. Planning zone visits and meetings
5. Membership changes
6. Working with other boards and committees. Recommendations to the congregation's voters assembly
7. Training in elders' skills
8. Identifying specific tasks and assignments to be completed by the next meeting
9. Next meeting date, time, and place

Confronting the Challenge

As you answer the following questions you will be moving toward the completion of the goals for this session.

1. What do your congregation's constitution and bylaws say about the goals and functions of your board of elders? Compare the expectations of your congregation with those quoted in the section "What's a Congregation to Do?"

_____

_____

2. Summarize in a brief paragraph what you think your congregation expects of you as an elder.

_____

_____

3. Write two advantages and two disadvantages of subcommittees for your board of elders. Discuss at least one way to facilitate more effectively the work of your board.

_____

_____

4. Discuss the following case study. Simulate conversations and actions by elders which lead to a God-pleasing conclusion.

_____

_____

Edward and Margaret Dryden, members of your congregation, have told their elder that every other Sunday they attend the services of the Christian Covenant Fellowship. They plan to continue this pattern. In other words, they will hold membership in both groups. They do not ask the advice of the elder. They simply say that they need the different types of worship and ministry both groups offer. They really want to continue their lifelong membership in the Lutheran Church, but they also desire the happy, free, and warm relationships of people in the Fellowship.

5. Write a list of at least four functions of elders zones for your congregation.

_____

_____

6. Agree on the items you will include in the next meeting of your board of elders. Identify them by the order in which you will address them.

_____

_____

7. Discuss a list of elders' skills you would like to see developed in training sessions within the next 12 months.

_____

_____

3.
Who Are These Elders?

Because they had joined the congregation just two weeks ago, Joan and Wilfred Shelburn and their high school-age sons, David and Bryan, hardly knew what to expect. The man who telephoned said that he was their elder. He asked whether he could visit with the four of them for about an hour on Tuesday evening. "You have been assigned to my zone," the elder said, "and I would like to get acquainted. I want to get to know you."

"He sounded nice," Joan said after hanging up the telephone, date and time of the visit having been confirmed. "But I wonder what he is really like. Who are these people the congregation calls elders?"

Some elders may answer, "We are ordinary people like you are. We are nothing special." But other members of the congregation will say, "Not everyone can be an elder. Only a person with unique, God-given qualifications can serve in this position of spiritual leadership."

Goals

The goals of this session focus on the qualifications of elders. By the time you have completed your discussion of the questions included here you will list the qualifications which Biblical authors ascribe to elders. You will also describe the elder as a person who cares, a Christian who communicates effectively in word and action the message of God's law and grace. You will compare the advantages of appointing elders with those of electing them. You will develop a plan for cultivating skills as Christian leaders who serve.

Biblical Authors on Elders' Qualifications

Jesus' apostles introduced the position of elders to the early Christian church. So, we can learn from them the qualifications first established for people in this office. The church selected elders because the apostles sensed a need for them. God had not dictated their appointment. Obviously, the apostles quickly discovered that God blessed the ministry of elders. The young church matured spiritually. God also increased its numbers.

We are interested in the competencies of the first elders, not simply as historical footnotes, but because through this information God also instructs us for our work. By His inspired Word, God helps us identify, enlist, and strengthen the elders the church needs today in order to achieve its mission. Congregations might well consider publishing widely among their members the qualities needed in elders so that appointments or elections can produce happy results.

Respected, Spiritual, Wise

The twelve apostles discovered the need for helpers when some poor Christian widows of Greek heritage were neglected in the distribution of financial assistance for food. To remedy this weakness in their Christian fellowship and welfare system, the apostles called a meeting of their fellow Christians and said, "It is not right that we should give up preaching the Word of God to serve tables. Therefore, brethren, pick out from among you seven men of good repute, full of the Spirit and of wisdom, whom we may appoint to this duty" (Acts 6:2-3). This new concept pleased the believers. They chose seven administrative aides.

The congregation searched for these qualities in the men they chose: (1) Do they have the confidence of their community because people witness their Christian behavior? (2) Are they filled with the Holy Spirit? (3) Are they filled with wisdom?

People who serve as elders or deacons should be recognized for their stable, balanced, Christian character and their willingness to serve Christ and their fellow human beings. How will others know that elders are full of the Holy Spirit and wisdom? They will know when they observe elders who discover, develop, and use the gifts the Holy Spirit gives them. They will also know when they perceive in elders the special gift of wisdom, that is, the skill of putting knowledge about God and His ways to work in the practical decisions of everyday life.

Qualifications Listed by Paul

In chapter 3 of his First Letter to Timothy the apostle Paul emphasizes the qualities needed in people who serve the congregation in any official capacity. First, he underlined the character of bishops or pastors, those ordained for public ministry. Then he marked the qualifications of unordained leaders, deacons or elders.

On the one hand, we see that the qualities desired in elders are not much different from those desired in all of us. On the other hand, we note that elders should be people with spiritual characteristics who are able to carry out more practical assignments than those given to pastors. Elders are to be Christian models who help to hold up and personally demonstrate to the whole congregation the noble goals it has chosen for its ministry.

Paul described the kind of elders or deacons congregations need today: "serious, not double-tongued, not addicted to much wine, not greedy for gain; they must hold the mystery of the faith with a clear conscience. And let them be tested first; then if they prove themselves blameless let them serve" (1 Timothy 3:8-10).

Let's examine these qualifications a little more closely.

"Serious." Elders are to be dignified or grave. That does not mean they should disdain humor or perpetually show a sad face. Rather they are to reflect in their conduct the weighty and important responsibility the congregation has placed on them. Often they will also chuckle and laugh about their own foibles and inconsistencies as they try to go about their heavenly Father's impressive business.

"Not double-tongued." Paul is the only New Testament author who used this word, and he used it only here. A double-tongued person is insincere. So to put it positively, an elder should speak with honest, artless intent, not out of both sides of his mouth, but with commitment to unfeigned truth.

"Not addicted to much wine." Surely this is obvious. But, not so fast! People willing to assume the added pressures of eldership in a congregation may be especially subject to the temptations of alcohol, which when abused, leads to alcoholism. A respected, Christian elder will seek to resist any attempt to compromise an alert, caring relationship with parish members.

"Not greedy for gain." Honest gain is a gift of God. Dishonest gain is a curse. Greed for gain is a mortal sickness because it is idolatry. Surrounded by the fascinations of big money, cars, houses, and even lotteries, elders are called to lives of honest work and unselfish sacrifice for the gain of others, not themselves.

"Hold the mystery of the faith with a clear conscience." A person's most priceless possession is confidence in the forgiving mercy of God. Paul stresses the need for an elder to have a good conscience about his own Christian convictions. Our only true inner security is in our trust that God has made us heirs of eternal life through the marvelous, mysterious, immeasurable work of His Son, Jesus.

"Tested first." Did Paul in these words instruct the church to examine candidates officially before they could assume office? Were they to pass an orthodoxy or character test first? We have no clear answer. However, Paul did require that the whole church declare that the candidate had proved over some time to be a person who "held the mystery of the faith with a clear conscience." His trust in God had been tested.

"Blameless." Paul expected the church to test the fitness of a person for the office of deacon or elder. A person who was above reproach, whose faith was secure, whose character was sound, who was not double-tongued, greedy, or an excessive drinker was a suitable candidate.

After calling for deaconesses (or the wives of deacons, we can't be certain which) to be "serious, no slanderers, but temperate, faithful in all things," Paul wrote, "Let deacons be the husband of one wife, and let them manage their children and their households well; for those who serve well as deacons gain a good standing for themselves and also great confidence in the faith which is in Christ Jesus" (1 Timothy 3:12-13).

While Paul never demanded that elders or deacons be married, he recognized that married leaders served as models to the congregation for relationships with spouse and children.

"Husband of one wife." A person who provides spiritual leadership in a Christian parish can not be a polygamist. He is called to be a faithful husband, committed to his wife for as long as they both live. He does not divorce her in order to marry someone else. Nor does he corrupt the marriage through an extramarital affair with any other woman. He lovingly cares for his wife, so that by God's grace she reaches the potential God has for her.

"Manage their children and their households well." An elder and his wife are partners in "bringing up their children in the discipline and instruction of God." As disciples of Jesus, parents and children together cultivate orderly obedience to God's will. They build a responsible and smooth-running household that not only carefully manages its own affairs, but also looks for ways to assist the families around them who are in need of spiritual and material support. Like the congregation to which they belong, the elder's family is a nursery for training in the knowledge and grace of our Lord Jesus Christ and in the new life-style He brings.

The Congregation's List

Informed by its study of God's Word the congregation may wish to develop and then publicize its list of qualifications for elders.

Your congregation's guidelines for selecting elders might include the following:

Desirable Qualities in Elders for the Congregation
As children of God through faith in Jesus, their Savior, elders
1. show a willingness to learn and grow in God's grace and the skills of serving Him and others;
2. demonstrate a faith which has been tested and refined through years of Christian experience;
3. faithfully participate in services of worship, the Lord's Supper, and small group adult Bible studies on Sunday and throughout the week;
4. pray regularly for the congregation, for its pastor and members, for their community, for all people, and for themselves;
5. lovingly work with their wives, if married, to strengthen their marriage and manage their households to fulfill God's purposes;
6. live personal lives which are above reproach;
7. exhibit mental and emotional stability;
8. demonstrate the ability to cultivate good interpersonal relationships, help people work toward solving personal problems, and live in love with those with whom they frequently clash;
9. show a deep commitment to the success of the congregation and the

pastor as measured by God's goals for them;
10. exhibit a willingness to risk for the sake of Christ and His Gospel and to forgive when frail Christians are unable to carry out all their plans perfectly.

From a Personal Perspective

Some members never see the congregation's list of desirable qualities in elders. However, most members are able in their own words to describe their ideal elders. Ask and you may hear something like this:

"The ideal elder, as I see it, really knows the purpose of our congregation. He wants us to grow. He believes the congregation should reach out and make new disciples for Jesus. He also believes that the members we already have are to help each other mature in their faith. In other words, a good elder is growth-minded.

"I also think he is convinced that this growth can happen only through using God's means of grace. So he gets excited about increasing the number of Baptisms of children and adults, participants in Holy Communion, family devotions, and private and group studies of the Bible. As a Lutheran Christian, he can properly distinguish between Law and Gospel because he is a good student of the Bible himself."

"My ideal elder is a person who cares about me, who openly communicates the love of God in his words and in his concern for people. He's tender, but he is also tested and tough. He's patient and prudent. He's gentle and generous. He's spiritual but he's good at helping us reach difficult practical decisions. He doesn't lose his temper. He doesn't pick fights. He's not out to be rich or famous. He treats all the members of his family with respect. He's got a good reputation in the community. "To sum up, he believes that his big job as an elder is in everything to glorify Jesus by loving us and everybody."

No person in the congregation perfectly matches the qualifications listed by Biblical authors and desired by the congregation and individual members. Yet, God, through imperfect elders, continues to do astonishing things. Lonely, guilty, terrified, or resentful people have become more comforted, free, confident, or forgiving. Caring elders, blemished but pardoned in Christ, deficient but empowered by the Spirit, have conveyed God's grace for the transformation. So God continues to bless this work of love by people whom the congregation sets apart for eldership.

Appoint or Elect?

Now we confront the question: How can a congregation move qualified people into the important position of elder?

Some congregations elect elders in the same way they choose other officers. A nominating committee identifies potential candidates, seeks their approval to be nominees, and upon their acceptance places their names on the ballot for the annual meetings of the congregation.

In this procedure the nominating committee studies the needs of the congregation and the qualifications it has set for elders. Then the committee keeps searching until it finds the people with the necessary qualifications to fill the needs of the parish. In the annual congregational meeting the assembled voters select by secret ballot the candidates they believe can best serve as elders for the congregation.

Other congregations ask all their members to nominate elders from a list of the male members of the congregation who are 21 years of age or older. Parish members receive a list of the duties and qualifications of elders agreed upon by the congregation, to help guide them in their nominations.

A committee of the current board of elders collects and tabulates the nominating ballots. The pastor and board receive the results.

Then another committee of the board with the pastor discusses with every person the members have nominated the qualifications and duties of an elder, assuring the nominee of the confidence the congregation has demonstrated in him. As a result of these interviews the current board of elders with the pastor appoints and reaches agreement with those candidates who are best able to serve the congregation as elders.

Both procedures have advantages and disadvantages. However, under God's blessing a community of believers can well use either to identify and put to work the gifts God provides in elders for the congregation.

A Servant Who Leads

Throughout his term, whether that be three years or nine years or longer, an elder learns to lead by serving. Such was Jesus' style of leadership. He came into our world from God the Father to serve, not to be served. Jesus said that whoever serves others is the most significant person in God's kingdom.

An elder is first of all a disciple of Jesus who learns by listening to the Savior speak in His Word. Then in serving others the elder has something to say. He has a message from God which can bolster those who worry, lift up those who are weary, and equip all for growing service to Christ.

Elders who serve do not pursue power and prestige. Rather they search for opportunities to lighten the load of those who are crushed by disappointments and ease the pain of those who are abused and oppressed.

Christian elders are moved by the love of Christ to a life of unselfish service in order that through the power of God's Spirit people may be liberated from the power of sin and set free for their own joyful Christian discipleship. Christian elders do not bind people with rules and regulations but declare them free in Christ to become what God calls them to be. The goal of elders in their service to Christ is that the people of God be free from the power of sin, Satan, and the fear of death so that they can lovingly worship God and care for the needs of their neighbors.

Confronting the Challenge

The questions and discussion suggestions which follow will help you move toward the goals of this session.

1. Discuss recent events in the life of your congregation and community from which your elders learned how (1) to follow the guidance of the Holy Spirit or (2) to build the confidence of the community in your parish or (3) to solve a problem with Christian wisdom.
2. Review the qualifications listed by Paul in 1 Timothy 3. How would you list them in the order of importance as qualifications for elders?
3. Compare the list of qualifications your congregation has established for its elders with the list in this chapter. Suggest changes which might improve both lists.
4. Evaluate your congregation's method of selecting elders. Describe the advantages and disadvantages of both electing and appointing them. Suggest at least one way to make your congregation's system more effective.
5. Describe the elder who leads by serving.
6. Ask the members of your congregation to help you develop an elders training program by suggesting in writing or personal interviews the qualities and abilities they want and need in their elders. Summarize their comments. Use them as a base for a year's program of elder growth.

4.
Elders Assist in Congregational Worship

What time is the service at your church?" Gordon Gruncastle asked his neighbor Milton Burney.

"I feel something is missing in my life," Gordon continued. "In fact, I've felt that way for some time now but have done nothing about it. I know what the problem is, of course. Two years ago I stopped going to church. That's what I am missing. I want to start going again."

Milton not only told Gordon the time of service at his church. He invited Gordon to come with him to worship the following Sunday.

Later when he told his wife about the conversation, Milton wondered out loud whether they would feel something were missing if they stopped going to church. That started an exchange of opinions and beliefs about worship that carried them through the evening hours. They also prayed together that God would awaken within Gordon a new joy over his salvation in Christ. Furthermore they asked God's Spirit to guide them to appreciate more fully their opportunities to worship Him, and especially to use His Word and sacraments more faithfully.

Goals

Milton Burney held no office in his congregation. Yet, he valued highly for himself and his family the worship life for which his congregation equipped him. The good record of attendance by other members of his congregation at worship services attested to the importance they all attached to Christian worship.

The elders of a congregation by their office reflect the concerns of the whole parish membership for creative and sound worship practices. The goals of this session include some of these concerns. In the time you spend together here you will identify the skills needed for private and corporate worship. You will also develop some guidelines for promoting, supervising, and participating in worship in homes, educational settings, and meetings as well as in corporate services, Baptisms, weddings, and funerals. As you discuss your prayers for and with individuals and groups, you will help one another both list the abilities you need and mature in

28

your abilities.

The Elders' Life-style

A Christian congregation looks to its elders to model Christian worship for all its members. This involves more than checking on the attendance of elders at Sunday services. Rather, Christian elders mirror for their fellow Christians a worship life-style. They yield their whole existence to God's service. They hear and respond to the apostle Paul's entreaty, "I appeal to you therefore, brethren, by the mercies of God, to present your bodies as a living sacrifice, holy and acceptable to God, which is your spiritual worship. Do not be conformed to this world, but be transformed by the renewal of your mind, that you may prove what is the will of God, what is good and acceptable and perfect" (Romans 12:1-2).

An elder finds meaning in his service to God in the prophecy of Zechariah. John the Baptizer's father blessed God for visiting and redeeming His people "to perform the mercy promised to our fathers" so that "we, being delivered from the hand of our enemies, might serve Him without fear" (Luke 1:73-74). God frees those who trust Jesus the Redeemer from the fears that would otherwise paralyze them. God rescues Christians from the forces of the enemies which oppose them.

A Christian elder rejoices that Christ has purged his conscience. As the author of the Letter to the Hebrews wrote, "For if the sprinkling of defiled persons with the blood of goats and bulls and with the ashes of a heifer sanctifies for the purification of the flesh, how much more shall the blood of Christ, who through the eternal Spirit offered himself without blemish to God, purify your conscience from dead works to serve the living God" (Hebrews 9:13-14). We all have an old selfish nature. But Christ makes us over into His new creation. He alone can do it. He shapes us through the forgiveness of sins.

Christ's sacrifice delivers elders from their dead works and initiates in them the desire to do the good works in which He has ordained that they should walk. By His redeeming love God sets Christian elders on a course of new obedience to Him as they learn to love their fellow human beings in Jesus' name.

"Therefore, let us be grateful for receiving a kingdom that cannot be shaken, and thus let us offer to God acceptable worship, with reverence and awe; for our God is a consuming fire," the writer of Hebrews instructed his readers (Hebrews 12:28-29). Aware of the awesome nature of God, whom all people must confront in the Day of Judgment, Christian elders gratefully praise God for their life in His eternal, immovable kingdom. With respect and veneration they undertake their responsibility to honor God above all things.

In their new relationship with God, Christian elders live with a dynamic that motivates their whole being and day by day influences their decisions. With the righteousness of Christ and the wonder of eternal life which the Holy Spirit generates, they put themselves into the service of Jesus, their Savior and Lord. It's their life-style.

Elders Work at Worship

Christians worship God because He has graciously led them to know and trust Him. By Word and Sacrament God has performed in them the miracle of faith in His mercy. To express this faith Christians are moved by God's Spirit to come together to praise God for His gift and to use what God has given to build up others in trust toward God. Not out of lazy routine or by legal constraint but because the Holy Spirit joyfully works in them, Christians put the gift to work in their worship.

The apostle Peter called for such action when he wrote, "The end of all things is at hand; therefore keep sane and sober for your prayers. Above all hold unfailing your love for one another, since love covers a multitude of sins. Practice hospitality ungrudgingly to one another. As each has received a gift, employ it for one another, as good stewards of God's varied grace: whoever speaks, as one who utters oracles of God; whoever renders service, as one who renders it by the strength which God supplies; in order that in everything God may be glorified through Jesus Christ. To him belong glory and dominion forever and ever. Amen" (1 Peter 4:7-11).

Only what we have first received from God in faith can we return to Him in acceptable worship. Our ability to honor God depends totally on His gifts to us. Yet, He does call us to serve Him and that requires work. So God's Spirit stimulates us to think about Him and His mission in Christ among us, to ponder intently on His saving work for all people, to decide how best to communicate to others the message of His grace and to assure people of His love on the peaks and in the pits of daily life.

If Christian elders are to help the members of their congregation worship, they must first acquire for themselves some skills in reflecting on, participating in, praying for, and in other ways supporting the Word and Sacrament ministry of their congregation. For the most part these skills come through partnership with other Christians in acts of family and congregational worship. However, formal classes and training clinics in worship will add to the skills elders acquire informally. New skills need not make worship any less spontaneous and happy. Rather, they can add to the joyful thanksgiving Christians bring in sacrifice to God, the Father of our Lord Jesus Christ. Faithful worship in itself leads to growth in the service of God.

The Elder's Private Worship

A Christian elder who daily invests personal time and effort in reading the Bible; who meditates on God's law, which uncovers his sin, and the good news that Christ Jesus forgives his sin; who prays for himself and others; and who commits himself to a ministry of Christian witness and love, not only grows in the knowledge and grace of God, but in power for his elder's task.

As he asks Jesus to open his heart to understand the Bible and receives answers to his prayers, the elder will say often with the Emmaus disciples, "Didn't my heart burn within me, while He talked with me, while He opened to me the Scriptures?" (See Luke 24:32.)

Private worship doesn't win for the elder a merit badge in Bible reading and prayer. Nor is it a character test by which an elder proves his mettle. Rather, private worship challenges an elder to receive the Holy Spirit's message in God's Word with a mind and heart that are eager to incorporate God's power into his life and work.

Led by the Spirit of God, a Christian elder is a son of God. He hears God say to him through the apostle Paul, "For you did not receive the spirit of slavery to fall back into fear, but you have received the Spirit of sonship. When we cry, 'Abba, Father!' it is the Spirit Himself bearing witness with our spirit that we are children of God, and if children, then heirs, heirs of God and fellow heirs with Christ, provided we suffer with Him in order that we may also be glorified with Him" (Romans 8:15-17).

Lifted up by God's Spirit in his personal devotions, a Christian elder reaffirms with Paul, "So we are ambassadors for Christ, God making his appeal through us" (2 Corinthians 5:20). And as he considers his servant role to others, the elder joins Paul again, "We beseech you on behalf of Christ, be reconciled to God. For our sake He made Him to be sin who knew no sin, so that in Him we might become the righteousness of God" (2 Corinthians 5:21). A Christian elder walks away from his private worship reassured of his reconciliation with God through faith in Christ so that in turn he may be God's agent of reconciliation for others.

Worship in the Elder's Family

In one sense Christians in a family worship all day long. They get up in the name of Jesus, eat, go to school or work, play, and enjoy some free time as children of God who have put themselves in God's employ. If someone painted a picture of a Christian family at worship, it well might show parents listening to their children with the love Jesus demonstrated when he took little ones into His arms. Or the painting could depict members of a family at the bedside of someone who is ill, or at the front door receiving in forgiveness a runaway daughter. As Christians put their faith to work in situations like this they worship God, bringing God glory by their acts of love and by their witness that God is good.

More frequently, however, when elders discuss family worship in their home and in those of others in the congregation they refer to a little more formal family event. When children are small a parent usually leads the family in Bible readings, discussions, and prayers. While an elder need not conduct every devotion in his family, certainly he will take the lead in many of them and will personally underscore the value of each one of them. When children grow older an elder will increasingly learn from them as they participate and sometimes lead in parts of family worship. Debating ways to live out faith in Christ through daily tasks becomes more exciting when differences of opinion arise among young people in the teen years and their "aging" parents. But this process in which an elder interacts both with God in the Scriptures and with the members of his family is the fundamental action by which he and his family are equipped for the mission to which God calls them.

As in private worship, sufficient time needs to be set aside for family devotions—and an appropriate place, too. Minutes during the early evening or immediately following the evening meal often seem suitable. Avoiding a rigid routine, an elder will still establish some order for his family at worship. Readings from the Bible, comments on what they mean for the members of the family, prayers, and spiritual songs are some happy ingredients.

At Meetings, Too

Should plenary and committee meetings of the congregation mix in Bible readings and prayers with resolutions and reports? One busy member who attended an evening meeting, knowing that he had to get up early the next morning for work, challenged the practice in his congregation. "Our meetings are too long already," he said. "We should just stick to business."

Worshiping the Triune God, Father, Son and Holy Spirit, *is* the business of Christians whenever they gather together. When we pray the Holy Spirit to guide us, He promises to answer our prayers with even more blessings for our congregation than He has already given us.

Christian elders can encourage Bible study and prayer in the meetings of the congregation by asking for them in each meeting they attend. They can also provide a worship handbook which suggests Bible readings and presents prayers which speak to the specific needs of the congregation and thank God for His unique blessings on the parish. Annual editions of such a handbook will keep fresh and alive the practice of worship in the meetings of the congregation.

In the Public Service

Some congregations ask their elders to help plan the congregation's worship program and to serve in public services as readers and helpers in the distribution of the Lord's Supper. Thus elders demonstrate that worship is a corporate activity, not simply the work of the pastor.

Unless the congregation appoints a separate worship committee, the board of elders normally assists the pastor, organist, and choir director in planning public services. The organizing principle for Lutheran congregations is the church year, which identifies a theme for each Sunday and the week which follows. The elements of a service usually contribute to this theme. The hymn of the week, the Communion hymn and others, the prelude, the readings, the sermon, and the postlude all help to make up a single, unified encounter with God, where Christians listen to, find meaning in, and respond in faith to His Word.

Private practice sessions may be needed to help elders feel comfortable in the role of a lay reader in the service. Studying the passages which precede and follow the reading will enable a person to present the selection with meaning. The elder's private meditation on the passage with the help of a sound Bible commentary will provide insights which make the reading enjoyable for the whole congregation. A committee of elders may be chosen to develop a set of guidelines for elders and others who serve as lay readers.

Elders who assist the pastor in the distribution of Holy Communion may also need a brief training. They need to know the correct names of the Communion vessels and how they are to be used with reverence. Some practice sessions will help elders ease into their first public appearance. A meeting with members of the altar guild can build the partnership which grows through joint service to the members of the congregation who come to the Holy Supper.

Should the congregation equip its elders to take the Eucharist to persons who are sick and shut-in? After the public service some parishes send their elders to people who are prevented from coming to the Lord's Table. The elders take the elements of bread and wine which the pastor has consecrated.

However, communicants are strengthened in their faith that Jesus presents His body and blood in the Holy Sacrament when they hear for themselves the words of institution. So the pastor himself more correctly consecrates and serves the bread and wine to persons in their homes or elsewhere when they are unable to come to church for the service. Elders certainly may accompany and assist him, if needed.

When the Baptism of infants is performed in the public service, elders may be called upon to represent the whole congregation. Then they witness openly that the congregation commits itself to help the parents faithfully bring up their children in the discipline and instruction of God. As they welcome the new member of Christ's body into the local company of believers, the elders promise that the congregation will pray regularly for the child.

Christian elders will also want to know how to conduct a Baptism in case of emergency, in the absence of the pastor. Pouring or sprinkling water on the head of the child, the elder says, "I baptize you in the name of the Father and of the Son and of the Holy Spirit. Amen." A prayer for God's blessing and the Lord's Prayer may be spoken if time permits. When an elder acts in an emergency, he should share the vital facts about the Baptism with the pastor as soon as possible so that the congregation may recognize and record them.

While elders may not act as leaders in marriages or funerals, they often help the pastor establish guidelines for these services. When a congregation's traditions and practices are carefully spelled out in print, a pastor is well prepared to discuss acceptable options with the couple to be wed or the family which grieves the loss of a loved one. The congregation's approved order of worship for such occasions can then be adapted to incorporate the interests of the participants while still meeting the standards of Lutheran worship.

Some congregations appoint one or two elders especially to greet visitors and prospective or new members as they arrive at church for worship. When they become better acquainted, an elder may assist a visitor or new member to meet and grow to enjoy the fellowship of other members of the congregation. This may be the most important function of a greeter, who not only warmly welcomes a person to the joy and edification of the service but who lovingly links people to one another for lives of mutual ministry through the week.

Ushers in the Service

Greeters and ushers form a team to provide an inviting context for Christians who assemble in church to worship. Sometimes ushers are organized, trained, and supervised by the congregation's worship committee. If no separate committee undertakes the task, the elders assume it.

In their service to Jesus, ushers learn the importance of maintaining easy accessibility to the building for all people, including the elderly and people with handicapping conditions. They alert the congregation's property committee to the needs people have when they arrive and find their places for creative and meaningful worship.

If the elders prepare instructions for ushers, they will include information about courtesies used in seating people before and during the service, how to use the lighting equipment, arrangements for additional seating, aiding people who become ill or have an accident, and how elders themselves can worship throughout the service. Concern for expressive and purposeful worship will motivate elders to train ushers to serve their fellow members cordially and attentively.

Elders Pray

Sometimes in a worship service or a committee meeting and many times in the family circle or in visits with sick and troubled members of the congregation, elders will pray. Not only will they petition God privately and silently; they will also publicly and out loud lead fellow Christians in thanking God and asking His blessing.

Small-group studies of prayer which actually prompt elders to pray aloud should be included in the personal growth section of elders meetings. The more elders pray under the guidance of God's Spirit in His Word, the more effectively elders will learn to pray for the whole church, for people in critical need, and for themselves.

Some elders begin their practice of public prayer by memorizing petitions which speak to situations and conditions which occur frequently. Then as they acquire more experience they grow in the ability to formulate their own praise to God and their own pleas for the relief only He gives in Christ Jesus, our Lord.

Elders expand their private and public prayer life by exploring together all that God does for us in worship, the meaning of God's presence for us in His Word and Sacrament, the impending return of Jesus, which generates prayer, and the work of the Holy Spirit Himself, who prays for us when we do not know how to pray as we should.

Included in a well-rounded prayer are praise to God for who He is and for His gracious acts of love toward us, confession of our sins as we repent and trust Christ's forgiveness, petition for God's rescue from the ills we and our neighbors face throughout the world, prayer for power to do His will in every circumstance of life, and thanksgiving, which acknowledges God's glory.

Worship Is Service

Christians worship because God continues to serve them in the proclamation of His Word and in the celebration of His Sacraments. Through the message of the prophets and apostles God reveals His redeeming activity in the life, death, and resurrection of Jesus. He also in the message conveys the saving power by which men, women, and children here and now are restored to eternal life with Him through faith. That's why the Bible readings and the sermon, as well as Baptism and the Lord's Supper, are such vital elements in the congregation's worship. Through all these God actually serves the congregation. In its worship the congregation serves God. In hymns, prayers, psalms of praise, and testimonies of faith the congregation brings its adoration to God, declaring His glory. That's why singing, confessing the creeds, and chanting spiritual songs are so important. Through them all the congregation serves God.

Confronting the Challenge

As you pursue the goals of this session consider especially the following experiences together:

1. Describe the worshipful life-style of an elder you admire.

_____

_____

What are his characteristics?

_____

_____

2. Identify two worship skills you would like to develop. How can your fellow Christians assist you?

---

3. What suggestions might the board of elders write into guidelines for the private and family worship of members of the parish?

---

4. Examine the worship tools your congregation provides or church officers use to lead devotions in church meetings. Make at least one suggestion for improving them.

---

5. Review the plans for the next three months of worship services in the congregation. Discuss with the pastor, organist, and choir director at least two ways to strengthen the services of worship as unified expressions of praise to the Triune God.

---

6. Discuss the congregation's guidelines for lay readers, the elder's role in the distribution of the Lord's Supper and the Baptism of infants, and wedding and funeral services. Identify changes which will enhance the worship of people who attend these events.

---

7. Evaluate the congregation's service through greeters and ushers. How can elders support their work?

---

8. Design a series of four training sessions to assist elders in their private and public prayers. Schedule the sessions for future elders meetings. What would you like to include in the sessions?

---

9. Identify the elements in worship in which (A) God serves us and (B) we serve God. Why are both vital?

5.
Elders Help Others Learn and Teach the Gospel of Christ, Too

Millicent Macleod always knew how to plan for Sunday morning. Since their first Sunday together as husband and wife some 15 years ago she and Stuart just assumed that they would worship in the early service at church. Then they would stay to study the Bible in an adult Class.

Their congregation tried to offer at least two Bible classes for adults on Sunday mornings and one adult Bible class during the week for 13 weeks in the spring and in the fall.

Sometimes Millie and Stu would attend separate classes because their interests differed. The congregation planned its classes to address a variety of the issues and needs their members confronted. However, most of the time the two of them explored the Scriptures together in the same class. This enriched their relationship because they could continue their learning in the conversations and decisions which followed the class. Sometimes they even accepted assignments which they pursued together prior to class so they could share their findings when the class reassembled.

Last summer the congregation's adult Bible class planning committee asked Stu to lead a class for six weeks on the subject "When Should a Christian Go to Court?" Stu accepted. "My elder's responsibilities keep me very busy," he said. "Others would be better qualified to lead classes in discussing other issues. But because of my interest and, I guess, some ability as an attorney, I believe I can make a contribution to the group examining this question."

"Normally, I think elders should concentrate on their job as elders," Stu observed. "We have more than enough to do. But participating in a Bible class is for me an essential equipping activity. Periodically, not every week, I can be a leader, too."

Goals

Learning and teaching the Word of God is the fundamental process by which Christian elders strengthen and instruct one another for their mission. The goals of this session focus on this process. As you read and discuss the ideas and suggestions which are included here, you will describe the nature and value of spiritual nurture in the elder's life. You will identify elements of teaching and learning the Gospel of Christ in an elder's home visits, in meetings of his zone, and in Bible studies by members of an elder's zone; also in on-site experiences and in Christian growth events for people who are engaged, married, single, single parents, unwed mothers and fathers, or divorced. You will also develop strategies for ministering with members of the parish who are weak or careless or straying from fellowship with Christ.

Elders Get into Their Bibles

Elders face a multitude of tests each day. So do their fellow members in the parish. More and more friends, neighbors, and public leaders in education, industry, and entertainment express open antagonism toward their Christian standards of ethics. A skepticism about their Christian teachings and practices moves like a turbulent wave through their community. Some people challenge Christian goals for marriage and family life as meaningless. Others ridicule all who go to church. "It's only a tradition," they say. The more vocal opponents attack basic Christian teachings by denying that people are inherently sinful and by rejecting the unending grace of God by which He freely declares sinners to be forgiven through faith in Christ. Some blatantly characterize the Bible as out-of-date and altogether obsolete. Some elders may feel that all their beliefs and their whole life-style are under enemy assault. And they are!

God through His Word builds elders up so that they can confidently face their tests and help fellow members do the same. As elders study their Bibles privately and in small groups God nurtures their faith in Him. He reminds them that He has transferred them from the kingdom of darkness into the kingdom of light in His beloved Son, Jesus. By faith in Christ God links Christian elders to Himself and to one another in the priesthood of all believers.

Brothers and sisters in Christ live and work all around elders and support them. God's Spirit Himself continues to guide and bolster them. He teaches elders the truth about themselves and their need for Him. He reveals the fullness of His love for them in every condition and situation of life.

The truth is that in Christ God saves and equips us for every good work. From Him we receive the power we need to cope and to conquer, to love and to serve others even as He in Christ has served us. His Word is indeed true. It will not return to Him empty. It will accomplish what He pleases. He will strengthen His people for their work in His name.

Elders who get into their Bibles discover again and again the peace of God that passes all understanding and the power of God that surpasses all imagination as a source for overcoming the spiritual attacks of Satan, our own flesh, and the world. In daily study of the Scriptures God instructs and empowers elders to put our Lord Jesus Christ first in their lives, wherever they are and in all they do. As they search the Scriptures elders will find meaning for their lives, help for personal and family challenges, and new strength from God's Spirit for the demanding tasks which their congregation has given them.

In Small Groups

Many congregations have set this goal for themselves: That every member participates in a public worship service and a small-group Bible study each week. That's a worthy target for all of us! We are refreshed by our celebration of God's mercy in Christ in the gathered company of believers which hears God's Word read and explained and receives Christ's body and blood under the sacred elements of bread and wine in Holy Communion. Participation in a weekly, small-group Bible study helps Christians develop skills in understanding and living out their new life in Christ as revealed in Scripture.

One of the large blessings elders receive through their study of the Bible in a small group of fellow believers is the assurance that they are not alone in their concern for the congregation. In the more intimate setting of a Bible class men and women of God can ask and answer questions which lead them to become mutually more effective as representatives of Jesus. They intentionally help one another become better church members and more able to handle conflicts, tensions, disappointments, and losses. They also learn a new trust that God will achieve His purposes through them. Their efforts in Christ will not be in vain.

Elders who regularly study the Bible in an adult group receive new ideas which would never come to them in their private study but which do emerge when partners in the class share their insight into God's message. Christians praying and working together achieve a better grasp of what God says in the sacred text. When a text is especially difficult and an elder may tire of trying to interpret a passage or a paragraph, a group of caring co-searchers can help him stay with it and eventually reap a harvest for his labors.

Such a cluster of Christian friends can also learn together how to develop self-control. If an elder is too quick to speak, he can learn first to listen. If an elder is afraid to speak up, he can learn to give his opinion and to share his feelings for the common good. While some Christians may view themselves primarily as spectators in the congregation, a small adult Bible class can help its members move out of the sideline bleachers into the actual playing field of service to God and to other people. If people are bored with their church membership, it's because they merely stand apart and watch. That is boring.

Home Visits

When an elder visits in the homes of the members of his zone he creates a learning, teaching, and nurturing situation. His overall purpose for personal contacts with fellow Christians is to become more sensitive to the issues and plights they encounter as God's people. Then they can together dig into the treasures of God's Word and their own Christian experiences to discover how better to follow God's directions and carry on His saving work. As they share what they learn from the Bible by God's Spirit, they ask, "What does what we have learned now require us to do? To what specific action is God leading us?"

A brief outline for home visits might look like this:

1. We listen to one another for clues to a common elation or enigma. What provides pleasure or what pains us as we observe how God works out His plans among us? What deserves our attention as God's people with a purpose?

2. We look to God's Word and the history of His church to speak a word of hope for solving a problem or a word of blessing to illumine a success. What statement of God's law diagnoses the real need among us? What relief from the Gospel sets us free to build on the gifts God has given us?

3. We ask God's Spirit to guide us toward decisions which will build us up in the faith and put us to work in advancing the cause of the Gospel of Christ in our congregation, our community, and throughout the world. To what work is God calling us? How does God's Word equip us to wear His yoke of service to others?

Initiating Home Bible Study Sessions

An elder may also want to help the members of his zone come together in home Bible study sessions. That's hardly a new idea. But it's a good one. From the time of Jesus' ministry on earth Christians have invited others into their homes for worship, Bible study, prayer, and fellowship. While some people feel threatened by classrooms and formal teaching, they feel free to participate in learning settings which appear less competitive. When Christians meet in a neighbor's home they relax in physical comfort and enjoy the informal climate that prompts spirited and caring personal interaction. More mutual concern seems to build up when Christians meet in the friendly, intimate context of a friend's living room or kitchen.

An elder can capitalize on the willingness of a zone member to host a home Bible study by inviting several other zone members to meet with the host to talk about an appropriate topic, book of the Bible, or issue which they might study together. Then they can also set dates and times. Active, maturing Christians will often commit themselves with enthusiasm to 60- or 90-minute weekly sessions through four to six weeks.

Ordinarily, an elder does not serve as leader for a home Bible study group. Rather, he helps select a person who will facilitate the group's inquiry. Different people have different qualifications for leading Bible study. The big question is: With this subject having been chosen, who can now best aid the group in achieving its purpose?

On-Site Experience

Sometimes the members of an elder's zone do not know the needs of other people in their congregation or community. They do not sense the opportunities for Christian outreach among people in day care centers, sheltered workshops, hospitals, technical schools, prisons, retirement centers, nursing homes, apartment houses, rehabilitated neighborhoods, and subdivisions. An elder who arranges for on-site experiences in these settings helps Christians acquire a better understanding of the anger and frustrations that plague so many people. Then Christians can better equip themselves through study and discussion to respond in love to those who live in their immediate vicinity and larger community. Families who through personal on-site experiences get to know other families can more effectively bear mutual burdens and offer concrete help in times of tension or crisis.

With Old and New Families

An elder's most taxing moments are often spent with families, old and new. At the same time an elder also discovers some of his biggest joys in working through what husbands and wives, parents and children endure in the "down periods" of their lives. That's why a Christian elder learns early in his work to keep close tabs on family relationships among the people in his zone.

Personal information about young adults, high school youth, and children should include current data regarding who is at home, in college, or in military service.

An elder will also try to cultivate up-to-date relationships with zone members who are engaged to be married, who have never married, who are living together or have become parents but have not married, who have children but are single parents, or who have been married but are now divorced. When a couple gets engaged or married, an elder can celebrate with the new family by showing concern and by alerting the new husband and wife to the pre- and postmarriage counseling and enrichment opportunities the parish provides through its pastor and others. When a couple wearies of marital stress and begins to think about a divorce, an elder may be among the first people in a congregation to become aware of the emergency. He can share with the troubled husband and wife his own Christian convictions about God's plans for marriage. He can also key them into conferences with pastors and other Christian professionals, as well as with couples who have successfully survived conflicts similar to their own.

Because they see the value, elders will participate in and be the first line of support for family life education events in the parish such as marriage and family enrichment weekends. They will also fund the attendance of their pastor and other church workers at continuing education seminars in new skills for counseling engaged and married couples and in referring them when necessary to appropriate agencies and other helpers.

Elders who persistently review the interpersonal and family relationships of the people in their zones can then help to shore up faltering marriages or perhaps even reconcile people who have suffered through a breakup. When the families of a parish grow vibrant and unselfish the entire parish becomes better able to respond to the cries for help that come from the homes of others in the community.

Weak, Careless, or Straying?

If a member of a congregation fails to participate in Sunday worship, neglects the Lord's Supper, makes no financial contribution, misses fellowship activities, and offers negative comments about church activities, who cares? In some parishes the answer is: hardly anybody! In other parishes the situation is worse: even the elders don't notice. Obviously, a congregation appoints elders for just such a task. They are to care about members who have become weak or careless in their partnership in the Gospel of Christ or who have begun to drift away from fellowship with other Christians.

Some will say the situation is not that serious. After all, can't a person trust God for eternal life through the redeeming act of Jesus on the cross and yet not be active in a local church? Perhaps. The test of faith is not church membership. However, only in unusual situations is faith sustained apart from close relationships with fellow Christians.

God calls Christians to bear the fruit of faith, and only the person who abides in Christ can produce good works. To abide in Christ He must nurture us by His Word and sacraments. If we sever ourselves from His means of grace, that is, if we do not keep reading and recalling His message of forgiveness in Christ; and if we do not repent, die to sin, and rise to life daily—the water of our Baptism signifies the drowning of the Old Adam—and if we do not receive the forgiveness God grants at His Holy Table, our link with Christ weakens. Eventually faith in Him dies.

What signals from the members of his zone should compel an elder to take notice? When do people begin to slip away? Normally, not one, but a number of accumulated factors and forces pressure a Christian. For example, a husband becomes seriously ill and is unable to work. So his wife finds a job. It's her first since they were married. Under new stress, she is less patient with the children, who are also more restless because they don't quite trust their father to manage the household while mom is at work.

Then comes the telephone call from the Sunday school superintendent. With his unpredictable outbursts Jonathon upsets his teacher and the other children in his class. The superintendent isn't certain whether Jonathon should continue in that class. Maybe a special group would be better for him.

If this telephone call is their only contact with leaders in their congregation over the past two years, Jonathon's parents may feel that the new problem is more than they can take. They may even decide that their relationship with the congregation is not that important. Why don't they let their family attendance at church slide for a while? Maybe things will improve later.

An elder who consults with the family only because their child no longer comes to Sunday school or the parents miss church has not yet uncovered their basic need. Their problems started long before the Sunday school superintendent called. Wasn't anyone listening when they first asked for help? Jonathon's mother brought him to Sunday school one Sunday and said, "I'm sorry we won't be in church today. My husband needs me at home. I'll pick up Jonathon right after Sunday school is over." Who heard her quiet cry? The finance committee read the note she once included in an offering envelope. It said, "We need to reduce our pledge. Please understand." Who listened to the pain in that little letter?

If no one at church hears these muffled but genuine pleas, Jonathon and his parents experience a new anxiety: Even the church doesn't care. Then the burden gets heavier. No one is helping. Eventually the family feels unable to cope with their situation. They withdraw. They avoid further contact with the congregation.

While it appears that the problem rests altogether with the weak, careless, or straying member, actually the congregation has often contributed to the member's anxiety. It has not responded with the love of Christ. So both the member and the congregation have failed when a person drops out.

Elders who visit with parish members in order first of all to listen to them help build reconciling relationships. We know from our own experience that we are more likely to trust a person who really hears us. Elders gain the trust of the people in their zone by actively listening to them. That's more than a superficial hearing. Polite social chatting does not go deep enough. To listen effectively an elder needs to learn how to help a person to unravel feelings, personal history, doubts, convictions, and the pain that accompanies the process of retreating from church fellowship.

Elders who too quickly jump into conversations to suggest what a drifting member should do can delay or thwart reconciliation. Elders, of course, eagerly desire a member's return to full fellowship, but first they show that they care, want to listen to the person's story, and are committed to helping that person work through the hurts, disappointments, and resentments connected with parish membership.

Learning how to minister with people who are withdrawing from the parish is a slow process. It takes time and training. Elders who can keep confidences, who have an authentic love for other adults, who want to develop new skills, and who are adaptable to change are best qualified to represent Jesus and His church in the effort to reclaim those who drift away.

Dr. John Savage, director of Leadership, Education, and Development (LEAD) Consultants, Pittsford, NY, has suggested that if elders will work hard over a period of one year they can expect a minimum one-third return rate of inactive members. His research indicates that *one half* of the people *who do return* will do so after the first call. The other half of the people who return require one call for *every* year they have been inactive. A board of elders which keeps a chart of calls made and people returned to fellowship will soon see the importance of patient, persistent, loving contacts with people who have become careless about their church membership.

Confronting the Challenge

Review again the goals you set for this session. Consider how the following will help you work toward them.

1. List at least two blessings God grants you in both personal and group study of the Bible. Describe what happens as you receive these blessings.

_____

_____

2. Ask for your congregation's plan for adult Bible classes for the coming year. Identify the classes you will attend. Plan your schedule.

_____

_____

3. Outline a home visit you will conduct this week. Describe the process you will follow.

_____

_____

4. Explore with the members of your zone which subjects they would like to discuss in a six-week home Bible study. Arrange with two families to rotate hosting the group. Contract with a leader through your pastor or adult education committee.

_____

_____

5. Identify an institution, organization, or home within your community where the members of your zone might gain personal experience in meeting people's needs. Arrange for a visit. Evaluate and share the results at a future meeting of elders.

_____

_____

6. By personal contact update your information about the family relationships of every person in your zone. List those cries for help you heard. Plan appropriate responses. Identify family life education events your congregation might sponsor over the next two years.

_____

_____

7. Discuss with fellow elders recent quiet pleas you heard from other parish members. What hurts did they express? Practice appropriate responses in active listening.

_____

_____

8. Case Study:
Tony and Geraldine Golden have not attended the Lord's Supper for 14 months. They say that they resent the recent stewardship caller who suggested that they pledge a financial offering to the congregation that exceeded by 10 percent any annual amount they had ever given before. They observe that they are thinking about joining another congregation.

Roleplay Tony, Geraldine, and two elders in a visit in this home. Evaluate the roleplay. Suggest ways to listen so that you can help reconcile.

6.
Elders Promote Witnessing to Christ, the World's Savior

Justin Dubois was surprised. The Lonnie Hallams family had agreed on the date he could come to their house for his elder's visit. But when he arrived he met two adults he did not know seated in the living room. They even looked as if they expected him. He was not a surprise to them.

Lonnie explained the situation. Their neighbors had just dropped in about 30 minutes before Justin's arrival. Lonnie asked them to stay because the Hallams and their neighbors had frequently discussed whether a person could really know that God exists and if He does, "What is He like?" or "Perhaps, what is She like?" as the neighbors put it. They admitted to being agnostics, but often talked about religious matters.

Tonight they welcomed the opportunity to meet with a church leader. Maybe they would hear something new. They liked the Hallams family and enjoyed conversations with Lonnie and his wife. But maybe an elder of a Christian congregation could open up different vistas for them. They warmed to the possibility of a challenge. Lonnie wondered whether he had done the right thing. He knew Justin as a loving and concerned Christian. But now the question was, "How effectively could Justin witness about Jesus to someone who is not a Christian?" Lonnie felt uncertain about his own ability. He hoped to learn from Justin.

Goals

Many Christians feel inadequate when confronted by people who do not believe the Gospel of Christ. They ponder how they, as disciples of Jesus, can speak clearly enough about Him so that another person by the power of the message will be drawn by God's Spirit to trust Jesus for salvation.

Do Christian elders know their Bible well enough? Do they know Jesus intimately? Will they ever be able to find the right words with which to approach the unique needs and conditions of the people they meet?

These are some of the concerns of this session. As you participate in the following study you will identify specific steps for presenting the good news about Jesus to people who are unchurched or "mis-churched" or "lapsed-churched." You will plan an approach to people that encourages meaningful conversation and confrontation, especially when they are apathetic and indifferent. You will develop a design for outreach through the elder's zone. You will also describe ways to receive and grow through the witness of other Christians to you.

Elders Are Witnesses

Just before He ascended into heaven Jesus promised His disciples, "You shall receive power when the Holy Spirit has come upon you; and you shall be My witnesses in Jerusalem and in all Judea and Samaria and to the end of the earth" (Acts 1:8). Jesus kept that promise. He empowered His disciples with His own energy and divine love. He moved them through the streets of Jerusalem, their home base, and then out into the neighboring countries. They were to achieve His purposes in the whole world. Jesus wanted people everywhere to know Him as their Savior.

Today Jesus continues to give the power of His Spirit to Christians so that they witness to what He has done and continues to do for them. Elders, too, are among these witnesses. From their own experience they testify how God brought them to faith in Jesus and has kept them in that faith. They openly acknowledge the gifts they have received from God. They publicly share the conviction that they and all people sin and thus earn the wages of death. They also publish the pardon of God who in Jesus covers our sin. They keep telling themselves and others that faith in Jesus is the Holy Spirit's gift.

Elders not only witness to God's activity in their own lives. They also tell about events through which God worked in other people's lives. They occupy key positions in the congregation for seeing evidence of God's gracious handiwork. Elders have intimate knowledge of God's power to convert, heal, and reconcile. They see God doing it all through the year. Their privilege thus becomes their opportunity. God equips them through their contact with others who have experienced God's transforming touch to demonstrate to still others that in His love for all people, God desires all people to be saved and to come to the knowledge of the truth. An elder who keeps a journal or a personal record of what he has seen God do for others will have a ready resource for witnessing to God's saving activity. It's so easy to forget.

Like the early disciples, modern elders are called to begin their Christian witness at home. They branch out from there. Recently a church leader confessed that he had missed something in his childhood. He experienced daily love. He also was brought to church and Sunday school. But he did not hear from his parents' lips the assurance of God's presence and care, of forgiveness and hope in Jesus, of power to overcome temptations and to show love to others. He regretted the empty silence. Recalling that unmet hunger as a child, he pledged as an adult and father to learn for himself, then to help others learn how to speak up, so that children hear the marvelous deeds of God at home, too.

Unless a fish is returned to water it squirms and squiggles until it exhausts itself and dies. It cannot live apart from water. So human beings are created to live in God. St. Augustine said that people are restless until they find their rest in God. Without God people exhaust themselves and die. Apart from God they are unable to find either peace or purpose for their lives. Only through a faithful witness to Jesus can anyone learn the joy of salvation and the spiritual wholeness that surpasses understanding. Elders are called by God to be such a witness.

The Opportunities Are Endless

Christian witnesses are eager to tell what they have seen and heard. They demonstrate how what God has done makes a difference in their lives. They stay alert for openings God presents to offer someone a word of encouragement, hope, peace, or reconciliation. They believe that God makes those opportunities. He wants the good word about Jesus to get to the people who need it. Through that dynamic message God adds to His church the people whom He is saving, all those for whom He reaches. They are beyond numbering, except by Him.

Even within a Christian congregation an elder's opportunities to share Jesus are endless. Some marital partners or parents or children of parish members are unchurched. Others in the congregation are unhappy because they feel "mis-churched." They think they might be more active back in the other church where they belonged before. Still others act as if they are unchurched because they have let their membership lapse. They are hardly ever named on a membership roster.

Whether unchurched, "mis-churched," or "lapsed-churched," people can be restored to the fullness of life with God. But it does not happen by wishing for it. Like all the rest of us, such men, women, and children must be called by God's Spirit to repent of their sin and put their faith in Jesus. This call of God issues from the lips of patient caring Christians. Announced again and again, sometimes over a long period of time, God's Word of judgment on unbelief and God's promise of grace for forgiveness in Jesus do not come without tenacious effort. Elders who have served through at least one term know what hard work it is! Yet, for exactly such reasonable, spiritual sacrifice God has initiated us into His kingdom. No one knows greater joy than to be a partner in the Gospel of Christ through which God gives a person a new birth to eternal life with God. Ask any elder who has experienced it!

Give Them What They Need

The evangelist John recorded the request of some Greek-speaking people at Palestine who came to worship God at the feast of the Passover in Jerusalem. They said to Philip, one of Jesus' disciples from Galilee, "Sir, we wish to see Jesus" (John 12:21). Maybe they did not grasp the full importance of their request. But by it they were seeking the "one thing needful." Jesus is the Christ, the Son of the living God. By believing in Him they would have eternal life.

The goal of Christian elders is to present Jesus to people so that by God's Spirit they put their trust in God through Him and serve Him as their Savior and Lord in the fellowship of His church. Moved by the same Spirit who compelled the apostle Paul, an elder can say, "For though I am free from all men, I have made myself a slave to all, that I might win the more. . . . I have become all things to all men, that I might by all means save some. I do it all for the sake of the Gospel, that I may share in its blessings" (1 Corinthians 9:19, 22-23).

To present Jesus to someone involves an elder in four basic activities. All of them grow out of the elder's compassion. Otherwise, though he speaks "in the tongues of men and of angels," but has no love, he is "a noisy gong or a clanging cymbal" (1 Corinthians 13:1). He is concerned for the whole person to whom he speaks. But an elder gives top priority to that person's continuing need for Jesus.

First, an elder in the words of Scripture and in his own words explains how God so loved the world that He sent His Son Jesus so that whoever believes in Him will be saved (John 3:16). He does not try to scold people into better behavior. Nor does he try to scare them into changing their ways. An elder tells the good news of Christ, who lived, died, rose to life again, and now prepares a place for us in heaven. Through that Gospel God rescues for eternal life everyone who believes.

Secondly, an elder shares his own faith in Jesus. He describes the power to change which Jesus brings to his life. He confesses his own joy in trusting that God forgives his sins for Jesus' sake. He points with confidence to his future because he knows that Jesus holds it in love for him. In *all* things Jesus works for his good.

Thirdly, an elder speaks specifically to the situation of his listener. How will the Word of God reach this person's fears, or guilt, or searching, or anger, or arrogance, or unbelief? Listening with care before talking too much, an elder senses the feelings which lie behind the words he hears. Then he tries to address the unique needs which those words and feelings reveal. Vague generalities do not confront, challenge, console, heal, or invigorate. But when a person listens to the narrative of God's love in Christ worded especially for him and his needs, he hears a faithful witness to Jesus.

Fourthly, an elder who presents Jesus summons a person by the power of the Holy Spirit to repent and believe the Gospel. A court summons requires action. "Appear in court, or else!" Jesus extends a much higher, more important summons. He calls people to change their minds about themselves. They must acknowledge that they have sinned against God and deserve His punishment. Jesus also calls people to turn away from every false hope for deliverance from that punishment. They are to put their hope in Him. So Jesus summons people to change their minds about God, too. How? By believing for themselves the pardon and peace with God that He has earned for them on His cross. An elder is God's agent of reconciliation who lovingly urges people to repent, thus dying to sin, and to believe God's message of forgiveness in Christ, thus rising to a new life.

Some Are Apathetic and Indifferent

People may explain why they are not active in a congregation in a variety of ways. What can an elder do, for example, when someone says, "My husband is on the brink of joining any day now. Then I'll come, too."

When a husband and wife together confess faith in Jesus as their Savior, God reinforces their love and care for each other. A Christian congregation will rejoice to see these two extend that care also to others who make up the community of faith. Christian couples provide backbone strength for a congregation's ministry. For that reason, they will be welcome.

However, God calls *each* person to repent, believe in Christ, and live the new life of service to Him *today*. A wife who genuinely cares for her husband will be better equipped to speak to him of spiritual matters when she has already committed herself to Christ through faithful church membership. Bolstered in the faith through her relationship with other believers, she will also be joined by them to show concern for her husband. She then has additional support for her witness and her prayers that God touch her husband with His converting power. Do they have young children? How vital it is for their spiritual lives, too, that their mother help bring them up in the discipline and instruction of God. Without her, they have no parent to guide them daily in their walk toward Christian adulthood.

Another person may say, "When I was a kid, I had to go to a Christian day school, Sunday school, vacation Bible school, and confirmation instruction. I burned out on religion!" An elder may need to listen longer to determine the meaning of a statement like that. Perhaps it's a shallow excuse that even the person who made it doesn't take seriously. On the other hand, some bad experiences in our childhood leave scars which do not easily heal. Adults try to avoid the pain they suffered when young. Who can blame them?

But the fact is, adults will not make mature decisions with a childish faith. God calls Christians to represent Him in today's world by showing His love and by participating in His mission. That requires seasoned judgment based on God's Word. We simply could not learn enough of God's Word as children to enable us to work through the complicated issues we face as adults. As surely as we confront new and more difficult moral and ethical problems, just as surely we need new insight into what God requires of us. So that we are not confused by new superstitions or hindered by obsolete human traditions, God frees us by the study of His Word in the power of the Gospel to play significant roles in our adult world. From Him we get the courage to contribute to solutions rather than merely create more problems.

What can an elder say when a person observes that he is as good or better, although he is not a church member, than many of the people who are in the church?

We are all saddened, aren't we, when people fail to keep their promises, when they actually are not what they appear to be. Obviously, Jesus was troubled by Judas, who betrayed Him, and Peter, who denied Him. However, He still yearned for their return to Him. On one occasion He explained that His church should be like Him in its attitude toward sinners. Some Pharisees asked, " Why does Your Teacher eat with tax collectors and sinners?" But when He heard it, He said, "Those who are well have no need of a physician, but those who are sick. Go and learn what this means, 'I desire mercy, and not sacrifice.' For I came not to call the righteous, but sinners " (Matthew 9:11-13).

The church of Jesus is not a museum which displays saints. It is a hospital for the healing of sinners. God really does His work in the church. Most of us know that through His Word and sacraments and in the fellowship of believers we are not only much better off but are much better persons than we would be apart from the church.

As Christian elders acquire more experience they are able to assist one another to listen actively to people who try to explain away their apathy and indifference to the Gospel of Christ. They will also learn from one another how to respond to such comments as: "We probably won't live near your church much longer." "Our community has so many churches. I can't choose which one I like best." "Your church expects too much. I could never learn enough to join." "Your congregation doesn't want anyone like me. I can't contribute anything." "You see that I can't get out. I could never get to church." "Can't you get a new pastor? I think your church could be a lot friendlier, too." "If your congregation is anything like the one where I last belonged, no thanks!"

Outreach Through an Elder's Zone

Through his zone organization an elder can increase among parish members an interest in reaching out to people who do not yet put their faith in Jesus. Through his own faithful witness to Jesus an elder stirs enthusiasm among fellow zone members for contacting unchurched children, youth, and adults. If he is eager to talk with people in his zone's area of influence about the joy of his salvation, others will soon join him. If he gains new skill in applying the Word of God to people who hurt because they are hopeless or who stagger under a load of guilt, the members of his zone will soon see how they, too, can learn to bring God's gracious relief to people.

Perhaps the best way to receive information about people who need God's rescue is to ask the members of the zone themselves. They often know or can learn the names of those on the block or around the corner who provide no Christian instruction for their children, or who have no personal Christian resources for making ethical decisions. Zone members know when a child is born, a couple is married, a person is injured or ill, or someone dies. At those times especially people often reveal their spiritual states. They also seem to be more open to conversations about the need for God's guidance and blessing. When an elder or his assistant shows an eagerness for gathering data about the spiritual needs of people in the community, zone members are more likely to share that information with him. Then he in turn can help harness the energies of the entire zone and others in the congregation to meet those needs.

A congregation may subscribe to a service which provides the names and addresses of new arrivals in the community. This information will also help an elder and his zone members extend the love of Christ to more people. The names of visitors to church services or other events may also be channeled to the zone in which the visitor lives.

In its meetings and through personal exchanges with its elder, a zone will want to keep outreach to others high on its list of priorities. Training sessions may also be on the agenda as well as Bible studies and workshops in personal witness. An annual assessment of how well the zone functions as an instrument for making known God's love for all people will uncover new ways to refine it for still more effective ministry.

Still Growing

Christian elders enjoy a personal privilege. They receive so much support for their work through the witness of fellow servants of the Gospel of Christ. As elders attempt to build up Christian community they receive in turn from the members of that community the spilling over of love. As they hear encouraging words and experience unselfish care from their zone partners, they continue to grow in their ability to encourage and care for others in the name of Christ. As they are fortified by fellow Christians for personal crises of life and death, they learn better skills for helping others find in Jesus Christ their hope and salvation. Because they have been loved by God and fellow members of the body of Christ, elders can love those who look to them to be neighbors in a time of need.

Confronting the Challenge

The following questions and suggestions will help you pursue the goals set at the beginning of the session.

1. In one-on-one conversations with a fellow elder tell and then listen

to him tell the conviction you have about Jesus that is most vital for you.

_____

_____

2. List at least two reasons for keeping a journal of what you have seen God do in the lives of others.

_____

_____

3. Identify five persons who are related in some way to the members of your zone but who are not Christians. Plan a strategy which brings a Christian witness to each of them over the coming 12 months.

_____

_____

4. Describe at least four basic activities by which an elder presents Jesus to a person who does not yet trust Him. Roleplay with another elder a conversation in which you engage in these four activities. As him to be (a) a long-distance truck driver; (b) a divorced mother of three teenage children; (c) a former Sunday school teacher who has abandoned the church; or (d) a police officer who walks an inner-city beat.

_____

_____

5. As a group write on a chalkboard or newsprint comments of apathy, indifference, or excuse which you have heard within the last six months. Compare them with those listed in this session. Suggest how to both listen and respond to people who make them.

_____

_____

6. Outline a system in which your zone can gather and share information about and follow up with calls on people who live within zone boundaries but have not yet tasted God's goodness in Christ.

_____

_____

7. Tell the experience you remember best in which the witness of another person strengthened you. What did you learn about Christian sharing?

_____

_____

7.
Elders Equip Servants of Jesus, the Compassionate Lord

Mateo Madera was surprised. He thought he knew the people from his congregation who lived in the immediate community. For example, he was certain he could name the members of the Bob Nickermann family.

What shocked him was the pastor's comment that the congregation was beginning a new program of advocacy for disabled people. He said Bob Nickermann started it all with a request for some Christian education materials for his son who was mentally retarded. Bob hoped that one day his son could be instructed for his first Communion and readied for the rite of confirmation.

Mateo was a little ashamed. He had not been aware that young Tim Nickermann would respond best to the teaching of the Gospel at home and in a class where special attention could be given to his needs. He wondered how many other people had physical, emotional, or social needs of which he and others in the elders zone were unaware.

Goals

Mateo confronted the same dilemma we all face. How can we respond to people when we hardly know them? How can we discover their need and then be partners with them in meeting it?

Elders in a Christian congregation can assist fellow members in their compassionate service for and with one another. As you continue through the following pages, you will develop guidelines for visits with people who are sick at home or in the hospital or who are shut in with long-term illnesses. You will identify ways to counsel the dying and comfort people who grieve the loss of a loved one. You will learn how to assist and to refer to other sources of help in your community those who are without jobs, between jobs, disabled, poor, hungry, homeless, or forgotten.

Servants of Jesus

Because they are first servants of Jesus, elders for a Christian congregation serve others. They learn from Jesus in humility to count others better than themselves. They begin to look out not only for their own interests but for the interests of others.

To this mind of Christ the apostle Paul urged the Christians at Philippi. He wrote, "Have this mind among yourselves, which is yours in Christ Jesus, who, though He was in the form of God did not count equality with God a thing to be grasped, but emptied Himself, taking the form of a servant, being born in the likeness of men. And being found in human form He humbled Himself and became obedient unto death, even death on a cross. Therefore God has highly exalted Him and bestowed on Him the name which is above every name, that at the name of Jesus every knee should bow, in heaven and on earth and under the earth, and every tongue confess that Jesus Christ is Lord, to the glory of God the Father" (Philippians 2:5-11).

That they may identify with people who have been abused, who are handicapped, or who are hungry and neglected, God displaces conceit and selfishness in Christian elders with humility and the willingness to make sacrifices. That was Jesus' life-style. He resisted the temptation to act as if because He is God He is above everyone. Instead, as God's Servant, the promised Messiah, He was "despised and rejected," "a man of sorrows and acquainted with grief." "He was wounded for our transgressions, He was bruised for our iniquities; upon Him was the chastisement that made us whole, and with His stripes we are healed" (Isaiah 53:5).

Jesus now empowers us by His love to put to work the new mind He has given us by faith in His sacrifice for us. This new mind is a whole new set of desires and a new commitment of our will to His purposes for us. Paul further explained to the Colossians: "If then you have been raised with Christ, seek the things that are above, where Christ is, seated at the right hand of God. Set your minds on things that are above, not on things that are on earth. For you have died, and your life is hid with Christ in God. When Christ who is our life appears, then you also will appear with Him in glory" (Colossians 3:1-4).

In Holy Baptism God's Spirit regenerates us with the life of God and creates in us the mind of Christ. Paul reminded the Philippians that they already had the mind of Christ. So do Christians today. By faith Jesus has made us His own. He lives within us. As Paul confessed, "I have been crucified with Christ; it is no longer I who live, but Christ who lives in me; and the life I now live in the flesh I live by faith in the Son of God, who loved me and gave Himself for me" (Galatians 2:20). As more and more Christ Jesus possesses us by the power of His Word, He renews in us His mind so that we willingly serve others. Our ministry of love to others is actually the expression of the creative, self-giving mind of Christ.

When Someone Is Sick

From the very first God's people have cared for one another in times of illness. In his general letter James wrote, "Is any one among you suffering? Let him pray. Is any cheerful? Let him sing praise. Is any among you sick? Let him call for the elders of the church, and let them pray over him, anointing him with oil in the name of the Lord; and the prayer of faith will save the sick man, and the Lord will raise him up; and if he has committed sins, he will be forgiven. Therefore confess your sins to one another, and pray for one another, that you may be healed. The prayer of a righteous man has great power in its effects" (James 5:13-16).

Those early Christian elders were probably mature Christians who themselves had been sick and who ministered with other people who had been sick, too. They knew the value of persistent prayer for themselves, for ill people, and for those who were tormented by a guilty conscience. They supported medical treatment with anointing and prayers for God's healing. They understood that such treatment under God's blessing brings healing as God answers the effective prayers of believers. While people *treat* one another for illnesses, only God *heals*. Out of His deep compassion Jesus made sick people whole again, cured the deaf and blind, and even restored the dead to life.

In the name of Jesus an elder seeks health and healing especially for the people in his zone. He frequently visits patients in a hospital or at home. His purpose is to share God's Word and to pray that God help the sick person in His daily care and according to His gracious will grant new strength and wholeness.

An elder will want to learn how best to bring the encouragement of God's Word to people in a variety of situations. What are some opportunities for which he might watch? Just before they have surgery, many people appreciate the assurance that God guides the surgeon. They take heart in the promise that fellow Christians in their zone will be praying for them while they are in the operating room.

During periods of recovery people may feel isolated and lonely. Brief visits or a telephone call from zone members will confirm that they are remembered and cherished.

If a person loses an arm or a leg, is badly scarred or deformed, or is made to feel less than normal, such a person may fear that other people will shrink back and not maintain their usual contacts. An elder and fellow Christians in the zone through repeated, caring visits can help such a person overcome fear, trust God's promises, and get ready for wider circulation again.

At the birth of a child most parents bubble with enthusiasm. However, some parents may experience increased anxiety, especially if the child will need special care and education or if the marriage or family into which the child is born is shaky. An elder visiting in the home after baby and mother return from the hospital can offer his own support and that of the zone to help parents feel more adequate for the challenge they face. Prayers to thank God and ask for His guidance will sustain that support.

An illness or accident may force some people into a new life-style. Heart disease, kidney deterioration, or cancer may compel people to change the way they think and behave. No change like this comes without pain or apprehension. It's tough! An elder who with the understanding of a brother in Christ can sit frequently or long enough to talk through and pray for the life modifications some people must make will be a brother to them indeed.

An elder emphasizes one basic fact in his visits with someone who is sick. Although our body may be weak or broken, God yearns for a strong and unbroken relationship with us. Although others may turn away and forget us, God turns His loving face toward us and remembers us with His loving kindness.

As an elder talks, reads the Bible, and prays with a person who hurts, they both experience God's healing. The God who saves them is the God who makes them whole. Salvation and healing are of the same divine process. So an elder's support for a person who is ill includes rejoicing in his/her salvation. Together they admit that of themselves they are powerless, separated from God by sin. They confess their sin. By their own fault they have ignored God and refused to trust Him. They recall for one another that God has pardoned their sin through the life, death, and resurrection of Jesus. Now by faith in Him they are God's people. They are no longer abandoned and alone. God is with them as they face their pain. Through faith in Christ Jesus they are now new people with fresh power to put themselves willingly into God's service. Spiritually renovated, they do good works lovingly to demonstrate that they are His new creation.

Once a young father who is ill, for example, senses that his elder understands his situation and shares some of his heavy load, new energies flow toward solving problems. At one time fear and loneliness immobilized him. Now the assurance that someone cares and that God continues to love him frees up his faith resources so that he can confront the difficulties, which now do not seem so huge.

How to help a person who is ill experience that liberation? Set aside enough time to listen. Hear whatever that father for example wants to say about himself, his wife and children, his situation. If you are too quick to tell him what he should do or not do or if you give the impression that you do not think he is able to make his own decisions, you stifle the healing process.

Listen also for the feelings behind the facts he shares. Eventually how he copes with his condition depends more on his attitudes, beliefs, and feelings than on what he knows. To the degree that he feels good about it he will move toward a solution.

Try to feel and think through the situation as he sees it. That's especially difficult when you have concluded that he has a faulty view of things. But you can best assist him when he believes that you accept his perspec-

tive as being validly his, the place where he is. When he believes that
you are genuinely with him, he receives new power to both endure and
press ahead.

Show that you are honestly trying to grasp the meaning and implications of his words. Without interrupting, reflect back to him what you
heard him say. At natural breaks in the conversation, lift up the ideas and
feelings which surfaced so that he can confirm or correct your response
to him.

We learn from Jesus how to listen. Luke records that the Savior
encouraged the two disciples on the road to Emmaus to share with Him
what turned out to be their crisis of faith (Luke 24:13-35). As He drew
from them their cry of anxiety, did they comprehend what was really
happening? Then Jesus began with Moses and the prophets to interpret
to them from the Scriptures all the events and teachings related to Himself. Jesus did not diagnose the pain for them. Nor did He criticize them
because they did not trust the word of the woman who channeled the
news that Jesus was alive. Instead He showed His eagerness to hear the
disciples out. First they put their anxiety into words. Then together with
them Jesus researched the Scriptures for words of truth about His mission. In that truth, by the power of His message that He was to suffer,
die, and rise again, Jesus restored them to life with God. It all started
because Jesus listened.

When Someone Is Dying

An elder may hesitate to talk with a person who is dying. Does Mrs.
Manley fully know her situation or has she not yet been told that death
is near? An elder may feel especially uneasy if he believes he is the only
visitor who approaches the subject with her.

On the other hand, a dying person may be reluctant to talk with an
elder. Perhaps he will get "pushy" and press for a full and final confession of sins. An elder may get so worked up emotionally at the prospect
of death that he upsets rather than comforts those whom he visits. If
members of a congregation know that about an elder they may refuse
to see him.

Obviously, elders and members cultivate their happiest relationships
when they share with one another the accurate information they receive
from doctors and pastors about life-and-death situations. Then elders can
emphasize the forgiving grace of God in our Lord Jesus Christ. In such
a setting a person who is dying will learn that he is free to talk or not to
talk about anything he thinks or feels. Eventually he may risk revealing
some of the fears, doubts, and apprehensions that trouble him within.
To pretend that no one dies is to prevent dying people from discussing
what pains them most. To accept the reality of death is to free a dying
person to be the person he is. Then real person to real person, elder and
dying Christian can grasp the gift of God which is eternal life in our Lord
Jesus Christ.

When Someone Grieves

What can an elder expect when someone in his zone experiences the loss of a loved one? Can he anticipate how that person will react to the death of someone who has been close? How can he help the fellow Christian who grieves?

Grief is the normal process by which Christians deal with important loss. When they accept this process they are less likely to be alarmed by their feelings about it. They will be less terrified by what's happening to them.

Some Christians may at first be unable to accept the death of a family member. Staggered by the loss, they can't even think about it. They may wonder why they don't feel worse about it than they do. They may need help to acknowledge that they are denying the death in order to try to cope with it. Gradually, they can be led to discover that they will not collapse or fall apart. They can in God's power and by His grace in Christ become fully conscious of what has happened and confront the loss.

A Christian who cries over the death of a loved one or friend is not experiencing an emotional breakdown, unless the weeping is excessive and extended. Tears release the grief. Jesus cried at the death of Lazarus (John 11:35). That caused people to say, "See how He loved him." Crying is a Christian way to express both love and sorrow. People who refuse to cry may build up forces that demolish them from within. If elders follow the apostle Paul's instructions, they will learn to "weep with those who weep" (Romans 12:15).

Often feelings of regret and guilt surface after a person has died. A daughter may rehearse what she could have done for her mother while she was still alive and feel depressed about her negligences. A father may regret the pain his harsh behavior caused his son, now dead. But he has no opportunity to ask for forgiveness. He can not hear the son's words of pardon. When such a daughter and a father confess their feelings of guilt to a loving elder, they can find healing in his message from God, "Be of good cheer. Your sins are forgiven. The blood of Jesus Christ, God's Son, cleanses you. By faith in Him you can go on with your heart at rest. Go in peace." (See 1 John 1:8-9.)

Elders support grieving Christians by assuring them that grief often continues for a while. Those who have lost a loved one may from time to time over succeeding months feel depressed, become preoccupied again with the loss, or experience guilt pangs. However, elders and other fellow Christians remain close by. They can confirm that the struggle for maturity in faith will bear fruit. The suffering child of God can learn by faith in Christ to face each new situation more confidently.

Toward what goals do elders press as they minister with grieving Christians in their zone? First, to give those saddened by a death opportunity to talk and pray about the loss they feel. To admit and express grief is to become ready for God's touch of soothing balm. Then elders can help a person grasp by faith the power of God in Christ Jesus to continue daily life, in spite of the loss. New challenges beckon. Will they be met successfully? Yes, when a grieving person discovers how to live without the person who died but with the beginning of new relationships. New contacts become open doors for service to others. Perhaps this is the most vital goal of all: that the person who in grief has gained a new appreciation for the love of God and fellow Christians begins to express that love to others. Growing in the conviction that Jesus died for all so that those who live can live not merely for themselves but for Him (2 Corinthians 5:15), a person is able to move back again into the mainstream of the serving Christian community. Becoming more active in loving and caring for others enables a person to recapture a sense of personal mission. Even more, this "wounded healer" becomes God's agent to comfort and build up in Christ others who have also been pained by the death of someone important to them.

Network Alert

An elder can reflect the compassion of the Lord Jesus by initiating an alert system in his zone. The purpose of this network is to identify those in the zone and in the community which the zone serves who need careful attention because they hurt in their body, mind, spirit, or interpersonal relationships.

The members of the zone themselves can most effectively signal needs throughout the network. Sometimes they will both sense a want and move to meet it as individuals and families. Especially as the zone lifts Christian caring to a high level of priority will its members become more tenderhearted and conscious of the afflictions and aches which distress their fellow human beings.

On other occasions the entire zone will want to know about a lack or injury which they can help remedy. That may call for a zone love-and-care group to receive the alert, share the necessary information, and manage a concerted response.

To provide a base of helpful resources for this group an elder may survey his zone to ask members two questions: (1) In what ways can you use some help in your family or home, or with transportation, or with special concerns? and (2) In what ways can you give help to others in their home, or with transportation, or with special concerns?

A small file containing this information can be tapped by a zone love-and-care group to help match resources with needs. Bonded by Christ's love for them and their attentive regard for one another, the members of an elders zone become a network to alert themselves to new opportunities for God's love to abide in them as they love not only in word and speech but in deed and in truth (1 John 3:18).

Time to Refer?

Some situations are so desperate or seem to defy solution for so long that the zone love-and-care group will need to refer people to community agencies. This does not mean that the zone abandons its members. Rather, it means that while Christians express their love in practical and concrete ways, they also try to link people in need with others who can help, too.

Another listing belongs in that file of the love-and-care group. It contains the names of local social agencies who counsel those who are unemployed, between jobs, disabled, poor, hungry, or homeless. They are also God's gifts to be utilized for the health and welfare of all the people whom God loves. A word of encouragement from an elder and the Christians in the zone who care can free troubled victims to seek and accept help from the variety of sources which God supplies.

Confronting the Challenge

As you consider the following questions and suggestions you will proceed still further toward the goals of this session.

1. Explain "the mind of Christ." Describe the attitude of elders who have the mind of Christ.

---

2. Identify special opportunities for an elder to concentrate on the health and God's healing of the members of his zone.

---

3. With a fellow elder alternate playing the role of a Christian who is recovering from a heart attack and a concerned Christian visitor. Discuss the feelings you had while playing the roles. Evaluate the "success" of the visit.

---

4. List and explain the elements of a Christian visit with someone who is ill.

---

5. Debate the advantages and disadvantages of talking about death with someone who is dying. Simulate an actual visit. Discuss how it could have been improved.

---

6. List and expand on at least two goals for elders who minister to Christians who grieve the death of a loved one.

---

7. Develop a network alert plan to help zone members respond to people's needs. Include a zone survey of needs and resources.

---

8. Prepare a small catalog of community agencies to be contacted when the need arises. Link specific needs with the agencies which can assist.

8.
Elders Build Up Congregational Fellowship and Support

Birdie Bristowe believes her congregation has it. She can not easily find the words to describe it. She thinks the Bible talks about it, but she has never actually studied with an adult group any sections of the Scriptures which treat the subject. She knows many new members look for it. What is it? Christian fellowship!

"I like the way the people at your church really pay attention to one another," Esther Kaye told Birdie after their families had attended a potluck dinner in the parish fellowship hall. "For them koinonia is a lot more than a word. You care about and support one another. I hope we can learn to do that in our congregation."

Esther's observations confirm Birdie's feelings. Her congregation's members do exhibit a genuine partnership in the Gospel of Christ. Not only do they sense it. They talk about it. They also try to strengthen it. They believe they are linked to one another through their faith in Christ. They consciously seek ways to brace that loving bond.

Goals

Elders play a vital role in building the spirit of Christian fellowship and support in their congregation. In this session you will list and begin to implement some goals which describe Christian fellowship. You will also develop guidelines for relating to youth and adult fellowship groups in the congregation, Christians in neighboring congregations, and parish members whose views conflict with one another. You will plan strategies for integrating new members into the life and mission of the congregation. You will work on some skills for dealing with the excuses and objections which sometimes frustrate fellowship. You will explain the value of the elder's leadership in the congregation's stewardship of toil, time, talent, and treasure.

What Is Fellowship?

Christian fellowship is more than feeling happy about our relationship with certain people. It goes much deeper than that. It's actually an expression of faith in Jesus. Christian fellowship grows out of a common trust in God's saving work through Jesus. When he gave thanks to God for the grace given to the Christians at Corinth, the apostle Paul told them that God would sustain them "to the end, guiltless in the day of our Lord Jesus Christ." Then he reminded his readers, "God is faithful by whom you were called into the fellowship of His Son, Jesus Christ our Lord" (1 Corinthians 1:9). Christians share in the eternal life of Jesus. By faith they participate in all that Jesus has done and continues to do for their salvation. They also share in the message of Jesus. Paul told the Christians at Philippi, "I thank my God in all my remembrance of you, always in every prayer of mine for you all making my prayer with joy, thankful for your partnership in the Gospel from the first day until now" (Philippians 1:3-5).

To live in fellowship with Christ is also to live in fellowship with others who live in Christ. Christians participate in a believing community. Through faith in Christ they are joined to one another, like the members of a person's body. They give to and take from one another in their partnership. Paul spoke of his close relationship with a fellow Christian when he asked Philemon to receive the runaway slave Onesimus, now also a Christian, back into Philemon's household. "So if you consider me your partner," Paul wrote to Philemon, "receive him as you would receive me" (Philemon 17). Paul appealed to Philemon that they were more than friends; they were brothers in the Christian faith. Because of this bond they could participate, trustingly and much more intimately, in each other's life.

Sometimes pain and testing can draw Christians together even more closely. Paul believed that God who had begun His work of faith in the hearts of the Philippians would "bring it to completion in the day of Jesus Christ." Then he explained, "It is right for me to feel thus about you all, because I hold you in my heart, for you are all partakers with me of grace, both in my imprisonment and in the defense and confirmation of the Gospel. For God is my witness, how I yearn for you all with the affection of Christ Jesus" (Philippians 1:7-8). In bad times as well as good, Christians give and take a share of one another's sorrows and joys. They provide positive help in times of need and lovingly join in celebration and congratulation in times of success.

Elders Promote Fellowship

If fellowship is an outgrowth of faith in Christ, elders promote fellowship among the members of their zone by cultivating stronger faith in the Savior. As Christians sense a more vital link with Christ they become aware of their growing interaction with all those who call Him Lord. Berating Christians for their lack of concern for one another does not enable them to become more selfless. Only the Gospel of Christ, powerful in God's grace, creates in people a commitment to one another in the love of Christ. Elders who support and encourage fellow Christians to read, hear, meditate on, and live out the Gospel of Christ are connecting these believers up with one another in a vigorous interlacing of God's love.

Especially at the Lord's Table Christians experience their oneness. Elders who seek closer fellowship among the members of their zone will encourage frequent participation in the Holy Supper. Together they will learn to trust God's promise through the apostle Paul, "The cup of blessing which we bless, is it not a participation in the blood of Christ? The bread which we break, is it not a participation in the body of Christ? Because there is one bread, we who are many are one body, for we all partake of the one bread" (1 Corinthians 10:16-17). Partaking of the body and blood of Christ in the Sacrament of the Altar, Christians both receive and testify to their unity with Christ and with one another in Him.

An elder's open house for zone members may help break the ice for people who need to test their unity with him and his family and with other neighborhood Christians. A backyard or patio in the summer or a family or recreation room during winter holidays is a comfortable setting for the informal conversations which can lead to deeper expressions of the bond Christians experience.

New members of the congregation, once assigned to an elders zone, may appreciate warm, personal attention and introductions to services provided by the congregation and the community. Perhaps a neighboring Christian or family by adopting or sponsoring the newcomers for 12 months can help integrate them into parish life. A two-year program of caring would make the effort even more successful. Incorporation into any new congregation takes time and does not occur without intention and effort.

Certainly an elder will want to alert members to the arrival in their zone of every new partner in the Gospel so that they may strengthen "the tie that binds their hearts in Christian love."

Fellowship Groups

Because it desires to reinforce the congregation's Christian spirit, the board of elders may be the group which can most effectively coordinate fellowship efforts. In some congregations a separate board does it. However, it's a natural for elders, too.

Elders in their regular meetings reexamine the needs of the parish, including those relating to fellowship. So they will also discuss such questions as: What fellowship groups will help meet the friendship and social needs of our junior high and senior high young people, young adults, men, women, and older persons? How can we help these groups organize and work around a Christian purpose? How can projects be coordinated so that organizations do not duplicate and waste energies? Do any groups conflict with the purpose of the parish? How can a group which has served its purpose be ended? Which new group is needed? How can the board of elders and all groups work together in healthy relationships so that God's people in harmony press toward the goals of the parish?

An annual evaluation will enable a board of elders and the fellowship groups of a congregation to improve their ministry of God's Word. On a scale of 1 to 10, from very poorly to very well, both members and observers might probe the following:

1   2   3   4   5   6   7   8   9   10
Very Poorly   **Very Well**

1. We have developed a clear statement of our purpose. We clarify it at our regular meetings.
2. Our purpose contributes to the purpose of our congregation.
3. In our meetings we work hard to accomplish our purpose, but we do not exaggerate business items.
4. In our meetings we also show personal care for the members of our group.
5. We involve all our members in setting goals and planning and implementing ways to achieve them. We know how our individual members want to participate.
6. We have arranged the settings for our meetings so that we are comfortable and interpersonal sharing is encouraged.
7. We know one another's gifts and abilities and we actively put them to work for Christ's mission in and between meetings.
8. We practice inclusive Christian ministry. We want to expand our fellowship so that all people feel welcome. We plan ways to grow in numbers, diversity, and quality of Christian interaction and service.

Elders support Christian fellowship when they help parish groups concentrate on who they are: people who are frail because they are sinners but new and growing in service through faith in Christ. As groups recognize and emphasize the worth of each individual member, they express the love of Christ for all. Where group officers keep open the lines of communication, informing all members of the agendas for their meetings, and share leadership roles in and between meetings, members of the group are more likely to become involved in its well-conceived activities.

Some congregations work closely with neighboring congregations in a circuit, an association, or in some other purposeful cluster. Through zone study, prayer, and service events an elder can help equip Christians for reaching out in Christian fellowship and love to other Christians in the community or area. Through such chaining of spiritual resources God supplies His church with new power. How does He begin? He changes attitudes. He creates penitent hearts and minds, willing to receive instruction from as well as give assistance to brothers and sisters in Christ from other congregations. A board of elders serves the whole church of God when it helps Christians relate in love to Christians from other traditions and with different histories. Of course, the board implements the policies for inter-Christian relationships established by the congregation.

When People Disagree

Elders soon learn that although Christians may belong to the same congregation they do not always have the same opinion about church work. In fact, they often disagree. They may even engage in frank conflict. Elders may be distressed by it but they should not be surprised.

Even the first disciples of Jesus disagreed. Only through an apostolic council did they solve the question of whether a person could be saved unless circumcised according to the custom of Moses (Acts 15:1). By confronting and working through the issue they finally told their fellow Christians that they need not be circumcised but that they should "abstain from what has been sacrificed to idols, and from blood and from what is strangled and from unchastity" (Acts 15:29). The apostles explained, "For it has seemed good to the Holy Spirit and to us to lay upon you no greater burden than these necessary things" (Acts 15:28). With the Holy Spirit's guidance and blessing, conflicts among Christians can be not only resolved but transformed into opportunities for personal and congregational growth.

To become more able servants, elders may need new skills in helping people to become reconciled to one another in Jesus' name. An annual skillshop in conflict resolution may be especially helpful to equip new elders and to keep experienced elders sharp in their conciliating abilities.

The following guidelines for managing conflict may serve as a foundation for developing the needed skills:

1. Conflict is as normal as it is inevitable. We are all sinful human beings. Because we do not love God with all our heart, soul, mind, and strength and we do not love our neighbor as ourselves, our frustrations erupt into conflicts.

2. Christians can resolve conflicts. Through the power of their faith in Christ and His forgiveness they can reach solutions. By patiently and thoroughly exploring acceptable alternatives they can come to mutual agreement.

3. Conflict is complex. Resolving one tension does not fashion a perfect family, committee, or congregation. The seed for new conflict often resides in the solution of an old one.

4. Jesus does not stir up trouble. Yet, He accepts conflict when it comes. Through conflict He leads people by His Word to trust in God's mercy and not their own righteousness.

5. Conflict can be a tool by which God stretches and strengthens us so

that we become better ministers of His Word.

6. People in conflict hurt because they care. Divisions cause pain. Actually, people are saying that they are not satisfied with what's happening. That can be helpful! They are calling attention to unmet personal and congregational needs.
7. The congregation and the community need examples of men and women in Christ who work through their conflicts and do not separate because of them.

Elders who successfully confront conflicts in the congregation usually help people work through questions like these:

1. What is the exact nature of the conflict? Can we agree on a description of it?
2. What attitudes do we need to help manage the conflict?
3. What personal and group behaviors will help?
4. Can we agree on the goals toward which we would like to move?
5. What are the specific actions we will take to manage the conflict?
6. What will result if we take no action?
7. What results can we expect from the actions we do take?
8. How can we build ongoing conciliation into the efforts to resolve this current conflict?

A collaborative style will best serve elders and others involved in conflict resolution. Although this style calls for elders to provide purposeful and firm leadership, decisions are reached by consensus. Those who make the decisions both participate in and accept ownership of and responsibility for them.

How do people in conflict move toward resolution? By committing themselves to *preparation, partnership,* and appropriate *period of time, participation,* suitable *processes,* and a *product* that is mutually acceptable. Preparation involves agreement on the guidelines and rules by which the conflict will be addressed. Partnership begins with consensus on who joins in the action. A long enough period of time is needed to discuss and unravel issues. All the significant actors in a crisis should be involved as participants. They also need to agree on the processes for solution which are the most suitable under current conditions. Finally, everyone contributes to a pleasing end product, reconciliation, by believing that they can do it, by the grace and power of God.

A Good Beginning

Helping new members make a good beginning will not only ready them for normal disagreements with other members; it will build the relationships needed in a caring congregation. Especially in some large, urban parishes new members may feel isolated, cut off from those who appear to be the old, stable members. Elders then have the opportunity to relate newcomers in these zones to the people who can give them a sense of belonging, to events which breathe a spirit of oneness in Christ and to service which confirms the new, selfless life they share in the body of Christ. The elders zone may be the most meaningful support group the congregation can organize to integrate new members into its life and mission.

Persons in a membership class may be assigned to an elders zone prior to their official reception. Then others in that zone may attend some of the sessions of the class to become better acquainted with the prospective member. In their own conversations between classes they may discuss some of the teachings and practices of the congregation which deserve deeper attention. Friendship with parish members will enhance all the worship, learning, and service experiences of prospective members.

Soon after the parish receives a new member a fellow member and neighbor in the zone might invite other zone members to an open house to introduce and honor the new partner in the Gospel. Brothers and sisters in Christ can then informally exchange views on the blessings, responsibilities, and challenges of church membership.

An elder may wish to schedule at least one visit every six months for a two-year period to ask new members how the parish can respond to their interests and needs. As questions pop up they will know how willing their elder is to hear from them. They will gain confidence in the congregation's ability to help them find meaning for their lives. Obviously the congregation's pastor will personally maintain contact, too. If the new family has children of preschool, elementary, or secondary school age, the elder may arrange for a person representing the congregation's Sunday, weekday, and vacation Bible school personally to invite the family to grow in Christ through these nurture opportunities. A couple who regularly attends adult Bible classes can enthusiastically witness to lives fulfilled through continuing education in the parish. By illustrating the variety of classes provided for adults they can demonstrate how the congregation plans classes and workshops which speak to the interests of the people who participate.

Zone members who belong to youth, men's, women's, or couples' fellowship can be contacted by the elder to share information about their group with each new member in the zone. Shared transportation can be an added stimulus to join an appropriate cluster of fellow Christians.

New members should immediately be incorporated into any of the zone's efforts to build up one another in worship, witness, and service to Christ Jesus. If they are neglected that first year, they may have great difficulty ever feeling at home. Cards and personal notes from other zone members for birthdays, anniversaries of baptisms or reception into the congregation, weddings, and funerals and other times of personal or family crisis will be more than friendly greetings. They will be links in a chain which binds Christians to one another in love.

A brief meeting of zone members in the late summer might consider the qualifications of new members to be nominated for the offices and board memberships which become open for the new year. With the encouragement of their zone some members might be more willing to accept nomination or appointment.

Integration into a congregation often occurs more quickly and effectively when one person or family acts as a sponsor or zone partner with the new person or family. As they pray for one another, research questions about the congregation and community, learn to know others in the parish, discuss ways to improve the worship services, reach more people with the Gospel, equip people for the ministry of God's Word, and respond to people's physical and social needs, both new members and sponsors can generate new excitement about their parish partnership.

Quick to Hear, Slow to Speak

James offers good advice for an elder who is disappointed when some people in his zone do not immediately take on parish leadership responsibilities. "Let every man be quick to hear, slow to speak, slow to anger, for the anger of man does not work the righteousness of God" (James 1:19b-20).

An elder who listens actively to the members of his zone discovers that they all have legitimate reasons in their own mind for either becoming more actively involved in the parish or for delaying their involvement. An elder serves Jesus by loving his fellow members as they are. Out of that love he can learn to hear their message with patience, and with a nonjudgmental attitude. As he listens by the power of God's Spirit, he can also develop the capacity to participate in both the ideas and the feelings they share. Compassionate hearing clears the way to understanding.

James addressed his readers, "my beloved brethren" (James 1:19a). God gave them to James as fellow members of Christ's family. They did not join the family solely by their own will. Nor could James add or remove them by his will. By His action God the Holy Spirit "called, enlightened and sanctified" them. He also acted to keep them in the one true faith. Elders who believe that God brings and keeps His people in the Christian faith will talk and live with them boldly and gently, participating in their common life in Christ.

One zone member may say, "I don't want to hear you talk about church work. I'll do the best I can. For now I hope you leave me alone."

An elder who responds may acknowledge that the Christian has many opportunities to represent Jesus to others in the family, on the job, and in work and play relationships. What's tough, however, is to set priorities. Here's where brothers and sisters in the faith can help. With a broad view of their mission Christians in the congregation can help a person sort out the opportunity or challenge which deserves top concern. This process may indeed result in the person doing the best possible and being left alone. On the other hand, working through priorities may result in a different course of action because the person chooses it with the counsel and support of fellow Christians.

One day the apostle Paul apparently would have been torn to pieces by dissenting Pharisees and Sadducees. The Roman tribune rescued him and brought Paul back to the soldiers' barracks. The Lord stood by Paul the following night and told him, "Take courage, for as you testified about Me at Jerusalem, so you must bear witness also at Rome" (Acts 23:11).

Paul accepted the new priority. Conducted safely through the night by Roman soldiers, he arrived at Antipatris and Caesarea. He moved from an old assignment to a new one. Of course, God intervened in this case. So Paul had a clear direction for the future. However, apart from that, Paul could also have concluded with the counsel of fellow Christians, "I'll do the best I can here. For now, leave me alone."

A zone member may say to his elder, "I have had good Christian training. I don't feel the need to attend classes or workshops in the zone or up at church. Those are for professional people."

The elder's first response could well be a word of appreciation and thanksgiving for the good training. That's a happy blessing from God in which Christians rejoice. The elder may then ask in what situations especially did the person put faith in Christ to work. Perhaps the zone member would be willing to share with others the new insight and strength gained from the experience. The elder may know of someone facing a similar situation for whom the account of the event would provide a real boost.

The Samaritan woman who met Jesus at the well of Sychar "left her water jar and went away into the city and said to the people, 'Come, see a man who told me all that I ever did. Can this be the Christ?' They went out of the city and were coming to Him" (John 4:28-30). John then records that "many Samaritans from that city believed in Him . . . because of His Word" (vv. 39-41). They said, "We have heard for ourselves and we know that this is indeed the Savior of the world" (v. 42).

Christians have a personal story to tell about how they came to believe for themselves that Jesus is indeed the Savior of the world. Elders can help provide opportunity for each person in the zone to tell how Jesus' story has been intertwined with a personal story on the way through this world to heaven.

Many Christians who never participate in the educational ministry of the parish nevertheless are still searching for answers to serious questions. A loving probe by an elder may uncover at least a couple of these unsolved concerns. The elder who lifts up these concerns to the congregation's adult education committee or parish education board can make a promise to the person who raised them. Every issue the Christian faces or every question raised by the Christian's attempts to relate faith in Jesus to the decisions of daily life becomes a subject for study in a practical Bible study program. The congregation's planning committee eagerly anticipates the expression of these issues and questions so that classes can be organized to address them. An elder can then invite the members of his zone to help plan and participate in the adult Bible class which reflects the crucial dilemmas they confront as they live as Christians in today's world.

As Good Stewards

The apostle Peter instructed early Christians in skills which helped strengthen their ties of fellowship. He reminded his readers that "the end of all things is at hand, therefore keep sane and sober for your prayers. Above all hold unfailing your love for one another, since love covers a multitude of sins. Practice hospitality ungrudgingly to one another. As each has received a gift, employ it for one another, as good stewards of God's varied grace: whoever speaks, as one who utters oracles of God; whoever renders service, as one who renders it by the strength which God supplies; in order that in everything God may be glorified through Jesus Christ. To Him belong glory and dominion forever and ever. Amen" (1 Peter 4:7-11).

A Christian elder in a congregation today rehearses for himself and the members of his zone how God has called them to be "good stewards of God's varied grace." They are "servants of Christ and stewards of the mysteries of God. Moreover it is required of stewards that they be found trustworthy" (1 Corinthians 4:1-2).

An elder is first a steward of God's Word, both Law and Gospel. God has entrusted to him the "management or administration" of that Word. It remains God's Word. A trustworthy steward studies, believes, puts into practice, and speaks to others the demands of the Law and the freeing promises of forgiveness in Christ through the Gospel. The elder's highest privilege as God's steward is to share God's Word with the members of his zone.

Out of his stewardship of God's Word comes the elder's commitment to be a faithful steward of his toil, time, talent, and treasure. Together with the members of his zone he reviews the opportunities God has set before the congregation to support with educational efforts and sacrificial funding the preaching and teaching of the Gospel of Christ throughout the world. Their mission is to all the earth's continents. Uniting with other congregations, a parish of The Lutheran Church—Missouri Synod contributes to eternal lifesaving work in more than 30 different countries. With a Christian world view an elder can keep his zone partners joined in Christ's mission with brothers and sisters in Christ in every place where Christ Himself comes.

Through its structure an elders zone can effectively inform members of challenges in the congregation and community to invest time, talent, and treasure in nearby ministries. A zone talent file can be a handy resource for helping to match needs and gifts to meet them. An elder happy with his own stewardship can best assist others to a life of Christian fellowship and mutual support.

Confronting the Challenge

In the questions and suggestions which follow, you will find more helps to pursue the goals of this session.

1. Compare the fellowship enjoyed by the members of your zone with one another with that which they enjoy in a civic club or precinct organization.

2. Describe two activities you could plan within the coming year to cultivate a sense of Christian fellowship among the people you serve.

3. List the fellowship groups in your parish. Discuss how their work may be more effectively coordinated and supported. Evaluate current or suggest new guidelines for this coordination and support.

4. Review the congregation's policies for relationships with
   a. congregations in your own circuit or denominational cluster; and
   b. with congregations and Christians of other denominations. Discuss how the policies may be clarified and improved.

5. What four guidelines are most useful to you as you develop skills for managing conflict? To what specific activities do you commit yourself over the next 12 months to acquire more skills in conflict resolution?

6. List at least three steps you will take to help integrate new members into the life and mission of the congregation.

7. List at least three reasons people have given within the last six months to explain their reluctance to get involved in church work. Roleplay with another elder a conversation by which you could respond to each.

8. Discuss at least two implications of the fact that an elder and fellow zone members are Christian stewards who build fellowship and support among Christians throughout the world.

9.
Evaluating Elders

Wҽ should have been doing it through the years," Andrew Stevens admitted. "But at least let's get started on it now. The time is right. The situation almost dictates it. We need to agree on some procedures to help evaluate the work of the board of elders."

As chairman of the board, Mr. Stevens knew the situation well. His congregation was interviewing candidates, preparing to engage a new pastor. Eight months ago their former pastor had moved to another parish. He had served long and faithfully and was ready for a new challenge.

In the interim the board of elders seemed to drift from one task to the next without a clear sense of purpose. They heard rumors that certain parish members had complained about inadequate spiritual services, but they failed as elders to seek more accurate information. Two elders had resigned but no one conducted exit interviews to uncover the reasons.

"No doubt about it!" chairman Stevens emphasized as he began the board meeting after Bible study. "We need to choose criteria by which we can evaluate ourselves and the ministry of our new pastor. Then at least once each year we can check out how well we are working together in reaching our goals. We can help our pastor assess his ministry and we can ask him to help us strengthen ours."

Goals

Most elders engage in some form of evaluation while they work at their daily jobs in agriculture, business, industry, or the professions. But some feel uncomfortable when asked to appraise the effectiveness of workers in Christ's church. The goals of this session speak to this apprehension. As you work through the following pages you will assess strengths and weaknesses in your congregation's job descriptions for elders and the pastor and other spiritual leaders or paid church workers. In view of the kind of elders your congregation needs you will outline a training program for elders for the coming year or for the current term of service. You will develop a plan which assists the congregation to sense current trouble spots and project future challenges. You will propose a design for annually evaluating the work of the board of elders and the pastoral and teaching team in order to strengthen your congregation's ministry of the Word of God.

Review Job Descriptions

Many congregations acknowledge the need to update the job

descriptions for their board of elders and their professional church workers at least every two years. A small committee can begin this work with interviews. The elders themselves will know how well their job descriptions actually explain what the congregation and especially the members of their zone expect of them. Spot checks with some elders and some parish members may reveal inadequacies or weaknesses in the descriptions. The committee can then recommend changes to the church council which oversees the development and adoption of job descriptions by the congregation.

As the committee also interviews the pastor and other paid workers for the parish, it may discover the need to change their job descriptions, too. New issues facing the members of the congregation often require a shift in emphases, time invested, and the skills needed in the pastors, teachers, deaconesses, and directors of Christian education and youth who serve the congregation. Once again recommendations for change go to the church council for approval by the congregation.

Gather Information

The purpose of evaluation is to gather information with which to make decisions about how services to the members of the congregation and the community can be improved. Self-evaluation by members of the board of elders can best be achieved when board members meet to evaluate their work as a whole. The chairman of the board of elders in private sessions may help each elder assess his work as detailed in the job description and determine how to strengthen in the coming months what he did in the past. In an exit interview at the conclusion of his term an elder may again review his job description and suggest ways his successor can improve the elder's services to the entire parish and especially to the members of his zone.

The items discussed in sessions two and three of this book will help the evaluation process move along to a successful conclusion. You may want to review those guidelines.

Evaluate Professional Church Workers?

In some parishes the board of elders is asked to cooperate closely with the professional or paid church workers and annually to evaluate their work. In other parishes a Professional Leaders Support Committee does the evaluating and shares a summary of its findings with the board of elders or the church council.

Before a committee meets with a church worker, it might request the worker to complete an inventory for self-evaluation. The worker may choose to share some of the information from the completed form with the evaluation committee. On the other hand, the inventory is primarily intended to help the worker to think through attitudes and perspectives on assigned tasks and to discover ways to cultivate new and better skills for ministry. Answers may vary from "usually" or "to a significant degree" to "hardly ever" or "have not considered it." If numerical values are assigned and tabulated, the totals are for the benefit of the person who makes the self-evaluation. They are not bargaining tools to persuade an evaluating committee to grant a higher rating.

Here are examples of some possible questions:

1. My goals and commitments agree with the goals and commitments of my congregation.

| 0% | 25% | 50% | 75% | 100% |

2. Parish members (_____ for the most part; _____ sufficiently to encourage me; _____ sometimes; _____ hardly ever) understand and appreciate what I am trying to do in my ministry with them.

3. I am able to change my ministry to respond more effectively to what parish members expect of me.

_____ most of the time   _____ sometimes   _____ rarely

4. I believe that the members of the parish and I have together developed a spirit as members of Christ's body which enables us to share openly our hopes, goals, strategies, disappointments, and achievements.

_____ consistently _____ with some breakdowns _____ no success

5. I have arranged for members of the congregation to give me accurate reflections and opinions to help me evaluate my ministry.

_____ often   _____sometimes   _____never

6. I believe the following areas of my ministry to be

Circle one from low (1) to high (5)

	Absolutely necessary	Required by congregation	In need of improvement	Enjoyable to me
	1 2 3 4 5	1 2 3 4 5	1 2 3 4 5	1 2 3 4 5
Teaching children	1 2 3 4 5	1 2 3 4 5	1 2 3 4 5	1 2 3 4 5
Marriage and family education	1 2 3 4 5	1 2 3 4 5	1 2 3 4 5	1 2 3 4 5
Leading worship	1 2 3 4 5	1 2 3 4 5	1 2 3 4 5	1 2 3 4 5
Speaking/preaching	1 2 3 4 5	1 2 3 4 5	1 2 3 4 5	1 2 3 4 5
Program planning	1 2 3 4 5	1 2 3 4 5	1 2 3 4 5	1 2 3 4 5
Personal counseling	1 2 3 4 5	1 2 3 4 5	1 2 3 4 5	1 2 3 4 5
Home visits	1 2 3 4 5	1 2 3 4 5	1 2 3 4 5	1 2 3 4 5
Continuing professional education	1 2 3 4 5	1 2 3 4 5	1 2 3 4 5	1 2 3 4 5
Ministry with sick, dying, or grieving	1 2 3 4 5	1 2 3 4 5	1 2 3 4 5	1 2 3 4 5
Promoting fellowship	1 2 3 4 5	1 2 3 4 5	1 2 3 4 5	1 2 3 4 5
Stewardship education	1 2 3 4 5	1 2 3 4 5	1 2 3 4 5	1 2 3 4 5

Equipping and supporting others 1 2 3 4 5	1 2 3 4 5	1 2 3 4 5	1 2 3 4 5
Leading adult growth groups 1 2 3 4 5	1 2 3 4 5	1 2 3 4 5	1 2 3 4 5
Meeting human care needs 1 2 3 4 5	1 2 3 4 5	1 2 3 4 5	1 2 3 4 5
Evangelism ministry 1 2 3 4 5	1 2 3 4 5	1 2 3 4 5	1 2 3 4 5
Administration and management 1 2 3 4 5	1 2 3 4 5	1 2 3 4 5	1 2 3 4 5
Organizing and presiding at meetings 1 2 3 4 5	1 2 3 4 5	1 2 3 4 5	1 2 3 4 5
Personal and spiritual growth 1 2 3 4 5	1 2 3 4 5	1 2 3 4 5	1 2 3 4 5
Services to the Synod-at-large 1 2 3 4 5	1 2 3 4 5	1 2 3 4 5	1 2 3 4 5
Community service 1 2 3 4 5	1 2 3 4 5	1 2 3 4 5	1 2 3 4 5
Other _____ 1 2 3 4 5	1 2 3 4 5	1 2 3 4 5	1 2 3 4 5
Other _____ 1 2 3 4 5	1 2 3 4 5	1 2 3 4 5	1 2 3 4 5

7. I have (_____ **adequately;** _____ **to some extent;** _____ **hardly ever)** reviewed my strengths and weaknesses.

8. The one significant area in which I would like to improve_____

_____

9. I have (_____ **not really thought about;** _____ **written down some preliminary hopes for;** _____ **developed specific steps in a plan for)** achieving concrete goals in my ministry over the next five years.

10. My congregation and Synod provide $_____ annually to encourage me to participate in some form of continuing education.

11. I consciously set aside periods of time for concentrated personal and professional growth experiences. _____ **annually;** _____ **when I feel I have the time;** _____ **when the congregation insists on it;** _____ **so far I have had neither time nor money**

12. Two specific objectives for myself and the congregation in the coming years are _____

13. Two long-range objectives for myself and the congregation are

_____

14. Four specific actions I will take to move toward my objectives:

_____
_____

Some congregations also ask a select number of members to answer the same questions the church worker answers. They, of course, complete the form from their perspective. After their answers have been tabulated and summarized, the board of elders or the Professional Leaders Support Committee may share the results in conversations with the church worker. Together they may then agree on what church worker and congregation will do to pursue the goals they have discussed.

Statement of Purpose

Annual evaluations of its church workers will also help a congregation test and revise its statement of purpose. Such a statement should answer basic questions about the congregation's mission. Precisely why does the congregation exist? How does God in His Word describe the work of the congregation? What are the functions of a New Testament congregation? What people should the congregation serve? What attitudes and skills should the congregation develop in order effectively to fulfill its purpose?

As the congregation rehearses its statement of purpose, it should also examine the specific projects and activities through which it tries to reach its targets. Goals without projects to achieve them are like fire without fuel to keep it burning. Both goals and fire will then fade. Projects which fail may call for an adjustment in goals. Or new activities altogether may be required in order to reach those goals which continue to be realistic, achievable, and consistent with God's plan for the congregation.

Some activities falter because the congregation expects the pastor to lead them. But he is busy at other tasks. Other members of the congregation may be overloaded, too. By carefully reviewing purposes, activities, and workloads among church workers a congregation learns the importance of setting priorities, carefully scheduling projects, and equitably distributing responsibilities among all the members.

Should elders or the church council hear regular reports on how paid church workers and lay committee chairmen and members are spending their time? Perhaps. By evaluating such information a congregation can determine whether too much time is being spent on some goals, and whether some goals are being neglected or even forgotten. Adjustments can enable a congregation to refocus its energies and resources on its purpose.

Continuing Growth

The elders who are best able to serve their congregation's purposes are first of all growing Christians. That's why many boards of elders set aside time for study, prayer, and training at each meeting and in sessions especially designed to challenge them.

At the beginning of each year an elder chairman who senses the need for spiritual maturation may invite each member of his board to target at least one knowledge, attitude, or skill area for growth during the coming 12 months. After summarizing the suggestions he will be able to propose three or four significant group training opportunities. For example, several elders may express an interest in developing prayer skills for their personal lives and for visits with people who are ill. Four sessions of from 45 to 60 minutes each can be designed to help elders pray more easily and effectively, privately and in groups.

Other elders may feel that they lack information about the doctrines of other Christian denominations. With more knowledge they could help the members of their zone both witness to and work more cooperatively with their neighbors in Christian service projects. As former members of other Christian churches become new members of their congregation, well-informed elders will more effectively ease the transition and help integrate the new members into the life and mission of their new church home. A short course on comparative symbolics will help elders feel comfortable talking with people who have made the change from one denomination to another.

A survey of the elders may reveal that some want to improve their ability to read, interpret, and understand the Bible, or to confront and overcome the fear of death, or to listen and respond more carefully in conversations with other people, or to counsel those concerned about marriage and divorce. Each of these needs and interests becomes an opportunity for study and action in an elders growth group.

As elders evaluate themselves and participate in the evaluations of pastors, teachers, and other paid church workers, they will discover other needs to be systematically addressed in the training sessions they propose each year.

Anticipate Trouble?

Elders do not normally look for trouble. Trouble finds them quickly enough. Members of the congregation who experience pain, disappointment, and suffering in their personal and social relationships look to their elders as well as their pastor for support and encouragement.

However, sometimes problems and conflicts simmer and come to a boil below the surface. Finally, when someone identifies them as trouble for the congregation, too much simmering and boiling has already occurred. Serious damage has been inflicted on the Christian fellowship. The bonds of Christian love have been eroded. The congregation has experienced a serious setback.

Elders can help their congregation make an early diagnosis of needs and tensions. To anticipate them is to prevent them from disrupting the congregation's mission. The healing process, applied early, can restore the congregation's level of spiritual energy.

Aware of God's design for their congregation, elders seek ways to improve its climate for ministry. They encourage a detailed reexamination of the functions of the congregation in order to ask, "How is the ministry going? How effectively is the congregation building up its members for their mission to one another, to members of their community, and to people in other nations in the human family?"

In order to explore what ministry means and then to make plans to do it under God's blessing, many congregations divide their work into five functions. Then they creatively assign committees or task forces to evaluate the past, remedy weaknesses in the present, and project improvements for the future. The entire congregation is enlisted with the committees to ask, "What are we doing well? What new opportunities challenge us to expand our ministry? To what special needs, problems, and concerns should our ministry respond?"

The five aspects or functions of ministry which warrant attention are worship, witness, teaching and learning, service, and fellowship or support.

A set of questions can easily be developed to help members of the congregation evaluate how effectively their congregation performs each function.

For example, one sheet for each of the functions might include the following:

A. A description of this function

B. A scale on which to indicate how well the congregation performs in this aspect of ministry

| 0 | 1 | 2 | 3 | 4 | 5 |

Totally Inept   **Moderately Well**   **Top Notch**

C. Reasons for the rating. Observations and experiences in the congregation. What lies behind the rating?

D. Suggestions for improving this function

E. Additional comments

When a sufficient number of parish members have returned their evaluation sheet for each function, a committee should be ready to tabulate the results and summarize recommendations for the attention of the whole board of elders or the church council. Charts and graphs may help to visualize the information which has been gathered.

The committee which draws conclusions may then propose programs and activities which (1) capitalize on and continue the strengths of the congregation in each function; (2) create ways to take advantage of the new opportunities which have been identified by members; and (3) speak specifically to needs and problems members have isolated for attention.

Elders who support careful review of the five basic functions of the congregation will help fellow members anticipate and work through potential trouble spots before they grow into inoperable cancers.

Schedule It!

Parish members frequently evaluate their elders, their pastor, and other church workers and aspects of ministry in their congregation in an informal way. Over snacks in their living rooms or after services out on the parking lot they tell one another what they like and don't like about their church. However, many of these comments are lost and no constructive changes result from the criticism.

Elders who evaluate their own work and who encourage systematic evaluation of other church workers and programs in a more formal way help make their congregation more effective. Periodic assessments gather data to help the congregation make decisions on how to improve its ministry of the Word of God.

"Schedule it," elders can say without fear when they have learned from experience the benefits of evaluating themselves and others.

Confronting the Challenge

As you move toward achieving the goals of this session the following exercises will help.

1. Carefully examine your job description as a member of the board of elders. Identify at least one change you might suggest to bring your job description more into line with what your zone members expect of you and what you have learned God has enabled you to do.

---

2. Share your job description with at least two other members of your congregation. Write down their suggestions on how to improve it. Discuss possible changes in your next elders meeting.

---

3. What changes do you propose in the job descriptions for your pastor and other paid church workers? Discuss with other elders.

---

4. Meet privately with the chairman of your board of elders. Discuss ways to increase your effectiveness. If you are retiring, suggest new helps for your successor.

---

5. If you do not have a Professional Leaders Support Committee, meet with your pastor and other paid church workers to discuss the merits of self-evaluation and mutual evaluation of your ministries. Agree on a set of questions to guide you. Schedule an evaluation for next year if you need to make a beginning.

---

6. Discuss your congregation's statement of purpose. How might it be revised? How does it help you test your congregation's effectiveness?

---

7. Ask each elder to suggest one issue or topic for an elders training session over the next 12 months. In your elders meeting summarize the responses and agree on three or four issues to be treated. Schedule the training events.

---

8. Design a one-sheet evaluation form for each of the congregation's five functions. Solicit responses from parish members. Summarize and visualize their replies. Develop plans to build on their suggestions.

---

9. Agree on a calendar for evaluations during the next 12 months. Schedule them now.

Appendix A

200 Bible Readings for an Elder's Personal Devotions

The Beginning—
Genesis 1 and 2

The Fall into Sin—
Genesis 3

Cain and Abel—
Genesis 4

The Flood—
Genesis 6–8

God Covenants with Noah—
Genesis 9

God Tests Abraham—
Genesis 22

Jacob Receives Israel's Blessing—
Genesis 27

Jacob's Dreams—
Genesis 37

Joseph Reunited with His Brothers—
Genesis 45

Jacob Blesses His Sons—
Genesis 49

Moses' Early Years—
Exodus 2–4

The Plagues—
Exodus 7–11

The Passover—
Exodus 12

Crossing the Red Sea—
Exodus 13

Food from Heaven—
Exodus 16

The Ten Commandments—
Exodus 20

The Golden Calf—
Exodus 32

The Ten Commandments—
Deuteronomy 5

Moses' Song—
Deuteronomy 32

Moses' Death—
Deuteronomy 34

Israel Crosses the Jordan—
Joshua 3

Jericho Falls—
Joshua 6

The Sun Stands Still—
Joshua 10

Gideon—
Judges 6–7

Samson—
Judges 13–16

Naomi, Ruth, Boaz—
Ruth 1–4

Samuel's Call—
1 Samuel 3

Saul Becomes King—
1 Samuel 10

Samuel Anoints David—
1 Samuel 16

David and Goliath—
1 Samuel 17

David and Jonathan—
1 Samuel 20

Saul Dies—
1 Samuel 31

David, Bathsheba, and Nathan—
   2 Samuel 11–12

Absalom Is Killed—
   2 Samuel 18

David's Song—
   2 Samuel 22

Solomon Becomes King—
   1 Kings 1

Solomon Prays for Wisdom—
   1 Kings 3

Solomon Builds the Temple—
   1 Kings 6

Solomon's Wives—
   1 Kings 11

Elijah, Ravens, and the Widow—
   1 Kings 17

Naboth's Vineyard—
   1 Kings 21

Elijah Taken to Heaven—
   2 Kings 2

The Widow's Oil—
   2 Kings 4

Naaman Healed—
   2 Kings 5

Joash Repairs the Temple—
   2 Kings 12

Hezekiah, King of Judah—
   2 Kings 18–20

Jerusalem Falls—
   2 Kings 25

Zerubbabel Rebuilds the Temple—
   Ezra 3

Dedication of the Temple—
   Ezra 6

Nehemiah and the Wall—
   Nehemiah 1–3

Esther and Mordecai—
   Esther 2–4

Job's Tests—
   Job 1–2

Psalms

Proverbs

A Time for Everything—
   Ecclesiastes 3

Immanuel Born to the Virgin—
   Isaiah 7

To Us a Child Is Born—
   Isaiah 9

Hezekiah's Illness—
   Isaiah 38

Comfort for God's People—
   Isaiah 40

The Suffering Servant—
   Isaiah 53

Free Refreshment for the Thirsty—
   Isaiah 55

Arise, Shine—
   Isaiah 60

False Temple Worship—
   Jeremiah 7

Jeremiah's Complaint—
   Jeremiah 12

A Righteous Branch—
   Jeremiah 23

The Fall of Jerusalem—
   Jeremiah 39, 52

Lamentations over Jerusalem—
   Lamentations

Ezekiel's Call—
   Ezekiel 2

Ezekiel a Watchman—
   Ezekiel 33

God Looks After His Sheep—
   Ezekiel 34

Valley of the Dry Bones—
   Ezekiel 37

Nebuchadnezzar's Dream—
  Daniel 2

The Fiery Furnace—
  Daniel 3

The Handwriting on the Wall—
  Daniel 5

Daniel in the Lions' Den—
  Daniel 6

Hosea's Wife and Children—
  Hosea 1

Israel's Repentance—
  Hosea 13–14

The Locust Invasion—
  Joel 1–2

The Day of the Lord—
  Amos 5

Locusts, Fire, and Plumb Line—
  Amos 7

Basket of Ripe Fruit—
  Amos 8

Jonah Inside the Fish—
  Jonah 1–2

Jonah in Nineveh—
  Jonah 3–4

Habakkuk Complains and Prays—
  Habakkuk 1–3

Man with a Measuring Line—
  Zechariah 2

Not Fasting, but Mercy—
  Zechariah 2

The Day of the Lord—
  Malachi 3–4

The Wise Men Visit Jesus—
  Matthew 2

John the Baptizer—
  Matthew 3

Jesus' Temptation—
  Matthew 4

The Beatitudes—
  Matthew 5

The Lord's Prayer—
  Matthew 6

Jesus Sends Out the Twelve—
  Matthew 10

The Parable of the Sower—
  Matthew 13

John the Baptizer Beheaded—
  Matthew 14

Jesus' Transfiguration—
  Matthew 17

Marriage and Divorce—
  Matthew 19

Jesus Enters Jerusalem—
  Matthew 21

Signs of the End Times—
  Matthew 24

Jesus Crucified—
  Matthew 27

Jesus' Resurrection and Commission—
  Matthew 28

Jesus Heals—
  Mark 1–2

Jesus Calms the Storm—
  Mark 4

Jesus Feeds the Five Thousand—
  Mark 6

Jesus Feeds the Four Thousand—
  Mark 8

Who Is the Greatest?—
  Mark 9–10

The Lord's Supper—
  Mark 14

Jesus in Gethsemane—
  Mark 14

Jesus' Death and Resurrection—
  Mark 15–16

Zechariah and Elizabeth—
Luke 1

Jesus Is Born—
Luke 2

Jesus Calls Disciples—
Luke 5

Jesus Raises the Widow's Son—
Luke 7

The Good Samaritan—
Luke 10

The Lost Sheep, Coin, and Son—
Luke 15

The Rich Man and Lazarus—
Luke 16

Zacchaeus, the Tax Collector—
Luke 19

The Last Supper—
Luke 22

Jesus Before Pilate—
Luke 23

Jesus on the Emmaus Road—
Luke 24

Jesus, the Word—
John 1

Water to Wine—
John 2

Jesus Teaches Nicodemus—
John 3

The Bethesda Healing—
John 5

Jesus the Bread of Life—
John 6

Jesus the Good Shepherd—
John 10

Jesus Raises Lazarus—
John 11

Jesus Washes the Disciples' Feet—
John 13

Jesus Is the Vine—
John 15

Jesus Prays—
John 17

Jesus Sentenced—
John 19

Jesus Appears to Mary Magdalene—
John 20

Jesus Reinstates Peter—
John 21

Jesus Ascends—
Acts 1

The Pentecost Event—
Acts 2

Ananias and Sapphira—
Acts 5

Stephen, the Martyr—
Acts 7

Saul's Conversion—
Acts 9

Peter Escapes from Prison—
Acts 12

Paul and Barnabas' Journey—
Acts 13

The Jerusalem Council—
Acts 15

Paul and Silas in Prison—
Acts 16

Priscilla, Aquilla, and Apostles—
Acts 18

Paul Before Felix and Festus—
Acts 24–25

Paul Sails for Rome—
Acts 27

Righteousness by Faith—
Romans 3

Peace with God—
Romans 5

Buried Through Baptism—
Romans 6

God Is for Us—
Romans 8

We Are Living Sacrifices—
Romans 12

Ministry with Weak and Strong—
Romans 14

Overcoming Divisions—
1 Corinthians 1

Sexual Immorality—
1 Corinthians 5–6

Marriage Guidelines—
1 Corinthians 7

Appropriate Worship—
1 Corinthians 11

Spiritual Gifts—
1 Corinthians 12

Love Is the Way—
1 Corinthians 13

Jesus' Resurrection—
1 Corinthians 15

Ministry of Reconciliation—
2 Corinthians 5

Give Generously—
2 Corinthians 8

Paul's Thorn—
2 Corinthians 12

Paul Disagrees with Peter—
Galatians 2

God's Promise Is by Faith—
Galatians 3

Free in Christ—
Galatians 5

Lift Each Other's Burdens—
Galatians 6

From Death to Life—
Ephesians 2

One in Christ—
Ephesians 4

Imitators of God—
Ephesians 5

The Armor of God—
Ephesians 6

Be Like Christ—
Philippians 2

Press On!—
Philippians 3

Christ Is Supreme—
Colossians 1

Free and Alive—
Colossians 3

Christ Is Coming—
1 Thessalonians 4–5

Keep Busy—
2 Thessalonians 3

Pray for Everyone—
1 Timothy 2

Faithful Elders and Deacons—
1 Timothy 3

Resist Love of Money—
1 Timothy 6

Strong in Grace—
2 Timothy 2

Ready to Do Good—
Titus 3

Jesus Is Superior—
Hebrews 1

Jesus, High Priest—
Hebrews 5

Jesus' One-Time Sacrifice—
Hebrews 10

Hall of Faith—
Hebrews 11

Hardship Is Discipline—
Hebrews 12

Joy in Testing—
    James 1

No Favoritism!—
    James 2

Tame the Tongue—
    James 3

Prayer of the Righteous—
    James 5

Living Hope—
    1 Peter 1

Chosen People—
    1 Peter 2

Wives and Husbands—
    1 Peter 3

Suffer as a Christian—
    1 Peter 4

Scriptures by God's Spirit—
    2 Peter 1

The Last Days—
    2 Peter 3

Walk in the Light—
    1 John 1

How Great the Father's Love—
    1 John 3

God Is Love—
    1 John 4

To the Seven Churches—
    Revelation 2–3

144,000—
    Revelation 7

Shouting Hallelujah—
    Revelation 19

The New Jerusalem—
    Revelation 21

Appendix B

An Elder's Prayers

For Guidance by the Holy Spirit

Heavenly Father, thank You for Your mercy. In love You sent Your only Son, Jesus, to become a human being in order to rescue me from sin and death. By Your Holy Spirit light up my heart with Jesus' love so that I may fully give myself in service to You. Guide me into Your truth so that I may know what to do as I seek to care for those to whom You send me. Grant Your power that I may not give up but rather continue with joy to do my job according to Your will. For Jesus' sake. Amen.

For Forgiveness

Hear my praise, gracious God, for Your forgiveness in Jesus Christ. I have sinned against You. I have sinned against my neighbor. I have not been faithful to my assignment. Because of Jesus' redeeming work, erase my sin. Rule my heart with Your new life so that I may be strengthened for more energetic witness to Your love for me and all people. In Jesus' name. Amen.

For the Congregation

I pray, dear Lord, for the members of my congregation. Thank You for the fellowship in Christ by which You have linked us to one another. Pardon our faltering and our failures. We have not kept our mind on the purposes You have given us. Instruct us by Your Word so that in cheerful harmony we may carry out the functions You have entrusted to us in Jesus Christ. Amen.

For the Minister

Lord of the Church, bless the minister of our congregation. Enable him to be a true teacher of Your Word. Put the power of the Gospel into his heart so that he always preaches and counsels in a way that is consistent with Your saving will. Grant me a heart that is willingly instructed, comforted, and emboldened by Your Spirit so that as I work with my minister I will do those things which glorify Your name and are helpful to me and my fellow members. For Your holy name's sake. Amen.

For the Board of Elders

Blessed Lord, You have distributed a variety of gifts to the members of our board of elders. Grant me and other members of the board grace to use these gifts in Your kingdom. We do not deserve Your goodness.

Yet you have called us not only to membership in Your kingdom but also to positions of responsible leadership in this congregation. Fill us with joy in the Holy Spirit so that what we do will always be acceptable to You and helpful in building Your church, for Jesus' sake. Amen.

For a Person in Trouble

Almighty and everlasting God, grant Your special blessing to _____ in this time of trouble. You alone can console people who sorrow. You alone can grant strength to the weak. As _____ and I cry to You for help in this distress, we trust You to hear us. Grant the wisdom needed to choose a course of action which eases the anguish and brings a solution to the problem. In the midst of this misfortune give peace in the knowledge that our sins are forgiven. Grant hope in the certainty that Jesus is our Resurrection. In His name we pray. Amen.

For a Person Who Is Sick

Lord Jesus, with Your healing grace look upon _____ . Relieve the pain and suffering. Restore wholeness. According to Your good pleasure give success to the work of doctors, nurses, and loved ones. Defend _____ from the dangers of depression and unbelief. Grant quiet confidence in You, our Health and our Salvation. Amen.

For Protection

Grant Your protection, O God. Unless You provide security I am in peril. By Your great mercy defend me from all dangers and bring me safely through the tasks of this day. Guide my steps that I may walk in Your way, eager to serve You; through Jesus. Amen.

For Power to Resist Temptation

You know my weaknesses, heavenly Father. I confess that I easily fall prey to temptation. Grant Your power that I may resist the allures of Satan, the world, and my flesh. Shield me with Your love so that no evil force may separate me from You. By Your Spirit help me constantly to obey You. For Jesus' sake. Amen.

For Patience

Loving God, I confess that I am impatient. I have difficulty waiting on You, accepting Your timetable. Help me to see that my time and schedule are in Your hands and You are perfect. Give me patience at all times so that I may trust You to work all things for my good; through Jesus Christ, Your Son, our Lord. Amen.

For Success in Service

As I prepare for this task, heavenly Father, I pray for Your guidance. Only by Your Spirit's power can I succeed. Grant that I may be sensitive to the needs and hopes of my partners in the faith. Make me an able assistant to anyone who looks to me to be a Christian neighbor. Crown my efforts with the blessings only You can provide. In Jesus' name. Amen.

Appendix C

Personal Pages for an Elder's Goals, Diary, and Records

1. My goals for the coming 12 months:
_____
_____

2. My long-range goals:
_____
_____

3. Notes for my elders diary:
January

February

March

April

May

June

July

August

September

October

November

December

4. Events scheduled with my zone members:
January

February

March

April

May

June

July

August

September

October

November

December

5. The roster of my zone and a record of my contacts with each unit:

Appendix D

Six Devotions for Elders Meetings

I

Today Your Mercy Calls Us (Lutheran Worship, 347)

1. Today your mercy calls us
   To wash away our sin.
   However great our trespass,
   Whatever we have been,
   However long from mercy
   Our hearts have turned away,
   Your precious blood can wash us
   And make us clean today.

2. Today your gate is open,
   And all who enter in
   Shall find a Father's welcome
   And pardon for their sin.
   The past shall be forgotten,
   A present joy be giv'n,
   A future grace be promised,
   A glorious crown in heav'n.

3. Today our Father calls us;
   His Holy Spirit waits;
   His blessed angels gather
   Around the heav'nly gates.
   No question will be asked us,
   How often we have come;
   Although we oft have wandered,
   It is our Father's home.

4. O all-embracing Mercy,
   O ever-open Door,
   What should we do without you
   When heart and eye run o'er?
   When all things seem against us,
   To drive us to despair,
   We know one gate is open,
   One ear will hear our prayer.

Come to the Waters *(Isaiah 55:1-13)*

1. Ho, every one who thirsts, come to the waters; and he who has no money, come, buy and eat! Come, buy wine and milk without money and without price.
2. Why do you spend your money for that which is not bread, and your labor for that which does not satisfy? Hearken diligently to Me, and eat what is good, and delight yourselves in fatness.
3. Incline your ear, and come to Me; hear, that your soul may live; and I will make with you an everlasting covenant, My steadfast, sure love for David.
4. Behold, I made him a witness to the peoples, a leader and commander for the peoples.
5. Behold, you shall call nations that you know not, and nations that knew you not shall run to you, because of the Lord your God, and of the Holy One of Israel, for He has glorified you.
6. Seek the Lord while He may be found, call upon Him while He is near;
7. Let the wicked forsake his way, and the unrighteous man his thoughts; let him return to the Lord, that He may have mercy on him, and to our God, for He will abundantly pardon.
8. For My thoughts are not your thoughts, neither are your ways My ways, says the Lord.
9. For as the heavens are higher than the earth, so are My ways higher than your ways and My thoughts than your thoughts.
10. For as the rain and the snow come down from heaven, and return not thither but water the earth, making it bring forth and sprout, giving seed to the sower and bread to the eater,
11. So shall My Word be that goes forth from My mouth; it shall not return to Me empty, but it shall accomplish that which I purpose, and prosper in the thing for which I sent it.
12. For you shall go out in joy, and be led forth in peace; the mountains and the hills before you shall break forth into singing, and all the trees of the field shall clap their hands.
13. Instead of the thorn shall come up the cypress; instead of the brier shall come up the myrtle; and it shall be to the Lord for a memorial, for an everlasting sign which shall not be cut off.

Prayer in Unison

Lord, be merciful to us. We are sinners. We have not been faithful elders for Your people. We have not been the cheerful servants of Your Word which You call us to be. We have put ourselves first. We have neglected the people in our spiritual care. Grant us Your grace in Jesus Christ. By His great act of love on the cross remove the guilt of our sin. By Your Spirit stir our hearts to obey You as faithful disciples. Enable us to be compassionate helpers to those with whom we minister Your saving message of forgiveness in Jesus Christ. Amen.

II

Leader: In the name of the Father, Son, and Holy Spirit.
Elders: Amen.
Leader: We bless Your name, O Lord.
Elders: Thanks be to You, O God.
Leader and Elders: O the depth of the riches and wisdom and knowledge of God! How unsearchable are His judgments and how inscrutable His ways! . . . For from Him and through Him and to Him are all things. To Him be glory forever. Amen.

Oh, How Great Is Your Compassion (Lutheran Worship, 364)

1. Oh, how great is your compassion,
Faithful Father, God of grace,
That with all our fallen race
In our depth of degradation
You had mercy so that we
Might be saved eternally!

2. Your great love for this has striven
That we may, from sin made free,
Live with you eternally.
Your dear Son Himself has given
And extends His gracious call,
To His supper calls us all.

3. Firmly to our soul's salvation
Witnesses your Spirit, Lord,
In your sacraments and Word.
There he sends true consolation,
Giving us the gift of faith
That we fear not hell nor death.

4. Lord, your mercy will not leave me;
Ever will your truth abide.
Then in you I will confide.
Since your Word cannot deceive me,
My salvation is to me
Safe and sure eternally.

5. I will praise your great compassion,
Faithful Father, God of grace,
That with all our fallen race
In our depth of degradation
You had mercy so that we
Might be saved eternally.

See the Father's Love *(1 John 3:1-10)*

1. See what love the Father has given us, that we should be called children of God; and so we are. The reason why the world does not know us is that it did not know Him.
2. Beloved, we are God's children now; it does not yet appear what we shall be, but we know that when He appears we shall be like Him, for we shall see Him as He is.
3. And everyone who thus hopes in Him purifies himself as He is pure.
4. Everyone who commits sin is guilty of lawlessness; sin is lawlessness.
5. You know that He appeared to take away sins, and in Him there is no sin.
6. No one who abides in Him sins; no one who sins has either seen Him or known Him.
7. Little children, let no one deceive you. He who does right is righteous, as He is righteous.
8. He who commits sins is of the devil; for the devil has sinned from the beginning. The reason the Son of God appeared was to destroy the works of the devil.
9. No one born of God commits sin; for God's nature abides in him, and he cannot sin because he is born of God.
10. By this it may be seen who are the children of God, and who are the children of the devil: whoever does not do right is not of God, nor he who does not love his brother.

Leader: With happy hearts we thank You for the gift of Your perfect love in Jesus, who brings forgiveness of sin to us and to everyone:

Elders: We praise You, Holy Trinity, and put ourselves at Your disposal.

Leader: For revealing to us in Your Word that You alone are the true God, Father, Son, and Holy Spirit:

Elders: We worship You, Holy Trinity, and ask You to use us in Your church.

Leader: For establishing in this place a community of Your love, a congregation of believers in Jesus:

Elders: We adore You, Holy Trinity, and consecrate ourselves to Your service.

Leader: For men, women, and children in this parish and throughout the world who witness boldly to Your compassion for all people and Your power to save all who trust Your mercy:

Elders: We exalt You, Holy Trinity, and pray that You will add more and more people to Your church through faith in Jesus, who came that everyone might have life in all its divine abundance.

Leader and Elders: Amen and Amen.

III

Prayer in Unison

In the name of the Father, the Son, and the Holy Spirit. Amen.
(Psalm 119, vv. 33-40)

33. Teach me, O Lord, the way of Thy statutes; and I will keep it to the end.
34. Give me understanding, that I may keep Thy law and observe it with my whole heart.
35. Lead me in the path of Thy commandments, for I delight in it.
36. Incline my heart to Thy testimonies, and not to gain!
37. Turn my eyes from looking at vanities; and give me life in Thy ways.
38. Confirm to Thy servant Thy promise, which is for those who fear Thee.
39. Turn away the reproach which I dread; for Thy ordinances are good.
40. Behold, I long for Thy precepts; in Thy righteousness give me life!

Glory be to the Father and to the Son and to the Holy Spirit; as it was in the beginning, is now, and always will be. Amen.

Live in Harmony *(Colossians 3:1-17)*

1. If then you have been raised with Christ, seek the things that are above, where Christ is, seated at the right hand of God.
2. Set your minds on things that are above, not on things that are on earth.
3. For you have died, and your life is hid with Christ in God.
4. When Christ who is our life appears, then you also will appear with Him in glory.
5. Put to death therefore what is earthly in you: immorality, impurity, passion, evil desire, and covetousness, which is idolatry.
6. On account of these the wrath of God is coming.
7. In these you once walked, when you lived in them.
8. But now put them all away: anger, wrath, malice, slander, and foul talk from your mouth.
9. Do not lie to one another, seeing that you have put off the old nature with its practices.
10. And have put on the new nature, which is being renewed in knowledge after the image of its Creator.
11. Here there cannot be Greek and Jew, circumcised and uncircumcised, barbarian, Scythian, slave, free man, but Christ is all, and in all.
12. Put on then, as God's chosen ones, holy and beloved, compassion, kindness, lowliness, meekness, and patience,
13. Forbearing one another and, if one has a complaint against

another, forgiving each other; as the Lord has forgiven you, so you also must forgive.

14. And above all these put on love, which binds everything together in perfect harmony.

15. And let the peace of Christ rule in your hearts, to which indeed you were called in the one body. And be thankful.

16. Let the word of Christ dwell in you richly, teach and admonish one another in all wisdom, and sing psalms and hymns and spiritual songs with thankfulness in your hearts to God.

17. And whatever you do, in word or deed, do everything in the name of the Lord Jesus, giving thanks to God the Father through Him.

Let Us Ever Walk with Jesus (Lutheran Worship, 381)

1. Let us ever walk with Jesus,
   Follow his example pure,
   Through a world that would deceive us
   And to sin our spirits lure.
   Onward in his footsteps treading,
   Pilgrims here, our home above,
   Full of faith and hope and love,
   Let us do our Father's bidding
   Faithful Lord, with me abide;
   I shall follow where you guide.

2. Let us suffer here with Jesus
   And with patience bear our cross.
   Joy will follow all our sadness;
   Where he is, there is no loss.
   Though today we sow no laughter,
   We shall reap celestial joy;
   All discomforts that annoy
   Shall give way to mirth hereafter.
   Jesus, here I share your woe;
   Help me there your joy to know.

3. Let us gladly die with Jesus.
   Since by death he conquered death,
   He will free us from destruction,
   Give to us immortal breath.
   Let us mortify all passion
   That would lead us into sin;
   Then by grace we all may win
   Untold fruits of his creation.
   Jesus, unto you I die,
   There to live with you on high.

4. Let us also live with Jesus.
   He has risen from the dead
   That to life we may awaken.
   Jesus, since you are our head,
   We are your own living members;
   Where you live, there we shall be
   In your presence constantly,
   Living there with you forever.
   Jesus, let me faithful be,
   Life eternal grant to me.

IV

Lord of Glory, You Have Bought Us (Lutheran Worship, 402)

1. Lord of glory, you have bought us
   With your lifeblood as the price,
   Never grudging for the lost ones
   That tremendous sacrifice;
   And with that have freely given
   Blessings countless as the sand
   To th'unthankful and the evil
   With your own unsparing hand.

2. Grant us hearts, dear Lord, to give you
   Gladly, freely of your own.
   With the sunshine of your goodness
   Melt our thankless hearts of stone
   Till our cold and selfish natures,
   Warmed by you, at length believe
   That more happy and more blessed
   'Tis to give than to receive.

3. Wondrous honor you have given
   To our humblest charity
   In your own mysterious sentence,
   "You have done it all to me."
   Can it be, O gracious Master,
   That you deign for alms to sue,
   Saying by your poor and needy,
   "Give as I have giv'n to you"?

4. Yes, the sorrow and the suff'rings
   Which on ev'ry hand we view
   Channels are for gifts and off'rings
   Due by solemn right to you;
   Right of which we may not rob you,
   Debt we may not choose but pay
   Lest that face of love and pity
   Turn from us another day.

5. Lord of glory, you have bought us
   With your lifeblood as the price,
   Never grudging for the lost ones
   That tremendous sacrifice.
   Give us faith to trust you boldly,
   Hope, to stay our souls on you;
   But, oh, best of all your graces,
   With your love our love renew.

First, Give Yourself *(2 Corinthians 8:1-15)*

1. We want you to know, brethren, about the grace of God which has been shown in the churches of Macedonia,
2. For in a severe test of affliction, their abundance of joy and their extreme poverty have overflowed in a wealth of liberality on their part.
3. For they gave according to their means, as I can testify, and beyond their means, of their own free will,
4. Begging us earnestly for the favor of taking part in the relief of the saints—
5. And this, not as we expected, but first they gave themselves to the Lord and to us by the will of God.
6. Accordingly we have urged Titus that as he had already made a beginning, he should also complete among you this gracious work.
7. Now as you excel in everything—in faith, in utterance, in knowledge, in all earnestness, and in your love for us—see that you excel in this gracious work also.
8. I say this not as a command, but to prove by the earnestness of others that your love also is genuine.
9. For you know the grace of our Lord Jesus Christ, that though He was rich, yet for your sake He became poor, so that by His poverty you might become rich.

10. And in this matter I give my advice: it is best for you now to complete what a year ago you began not only to do but to desire,
11. So that your readiness in desiring it may be matched by your completing it out of what you have.
12. For if the readiness is there, it is acceptable according to what a man has, not according to what he has not.
13. I do not mean that others should be eased and you burdened,
14. But that as a matter of equality your abundance at the present time should supply their want, so that their abundance may supply your want, that there may be equality.
15. As it is written, "He who gathered much had nothing over, and he who gathered little had no lack."

Leader: Holy Spirit, change us today.
Elders: Transform our attitude.
Leader: So often we want our own way.
Elders: Give us the attitude of Jesus so that we want to follow Your way.
Leader: We confess that we have lived for ourselves.
Elders: Retool us so that we live for Him who gave Himself for us.
Leader: We admit that the evil we don't want to do is what we often do in the weakness of our sinful self.
Elders: Give us Your new life so that we more frequently do the good You call us to do.
Leader: We acknowledge that we give in too often to temper and anger.
Elders: Reshape us by Your love in Jesus so that we give ourselves in sacrifice for anyone who needs us.
Leader and Elders: By Your grace, renew us, Spirit of God, that being dead to sin, we may become fully alive to Your purposes for us. Amen.

Believe and Tell (Luke 24:13-35)

13. That very day two of them were going to a village named Emmaus, about seven miles from Jerusalem,
14. And talking with each other about all these things that had happened.
15. While they were talking and discussing together, Jesus Himself drew near and went with them.
16. But their eyes were kept from recognizing Him.

17. And He said to them, "What is this conversation which you are holding with each other as you walk?" And they stood still, looking sad.
18. Then one of them, named Cleopas, answered Him, "Are you the only visitor to Jerusalem who does not know the things that have happened there in these days?"
19. And He said to them, "What things?" And they said to Him, "Concerning Jesus of Nazareth, who was a prophet mighty in deed and word before God and all the people,
20. And how our chief priests and rulers delivered Him up to be condemned to death, and crucified Him.
21. But we had hoped that He was the one to redeem Israel. Yes, and besides all this, it is now the third day since this happened.
22. Moreover, some women of our company amazed us. They were at the tomb early in the morning
23. And did not find His body; and they came back saying that they had even seen a vision of angels, who said that He was alive.
24. Some of those who were with us went to the tomb, and found it just as the women had said; but Him they did not see."
25. And He said to them, "O foolish men, and slow of heart to believe all that the prophets have spoken!
26. Was it not necessary that the Christ should suffer these things and enter into His glory?"
27. And beginning with Moses and all the prophets, He interpreted to them in all the Scriptures the things concerning Himself.
28. So they drew near to the village to which they were going. He appeared to be going further,
29. But they constrained Him, saying, "Stay with us, for it is toward evening and the day is now far spent." So He went in to stay with them.
30. When He was at table with them, He took the bread and blessed and broke it and gave it to them.
31. And their eyes were opened and they recognized Him; and He vanished out of their sight.
32. They said to each other, "Did not our hearts burn within us while He talked to us on the road, while He opened to us the Scriptures?"
33. And they rose that same hour and returned to Jerusalem; and they found the eleven gathered together and those who were with them,
34. Who said, "The Lord has risen indeed, and has appeared to Simon!"
35. Then they told what had happened on the road, and how He was known to them in the breaking of the bread.

All Depends on Our Possessing (Lutheran Worship, 415)

1. All depends on our possessing
   God's free grace and constant blessing,
   Though all earthly wealth depart.
   They who trust with faith unshaken
   By their God are not forsaken
   And will keep a dauntless heart.

2. He who to this day has fed me
   And to many joys had led me
   Is and ever shall be mine.
   He who did so gently school me,
   He who daily guides and rules me
   Will remain my help divine.

3. Many spend their lives in fretting
   Over trifles and in getting
   Things that lack all solid ground.
   I shall strive to win a treasure
   That will bring me lasting pleasure
   And that now is seldom found.

4. When with sorrow I am stricken,
   Hope anew my heart will quicken,
   All my longing shall be stilled.
   To his loving-kindness tender
   Soul and body I surrender,
   For on God alone I build.

5. Well he knows what best to grant me;
   All the longing hopes that haunt me,
   Joy and sorrow, have their day.
   I shall doubt his wisdom never;
   As God wills, so be it ever;
   I commit to him my way.

6. If my days on earth he lengthen,
   God my weary soul will strengthen;
   All my trust in him I place.
   Earthly wealth is not abiding,
   Like a stream away is gliding;
   Safe I anchor in his grace.

Prayer in Unison

Lord, we believe. Help our unbelief. Save us who trust in You.

We confess that we are often slow to put our faith in You. We have too quickly put our confidence in our own ability, in the power of money, and in the strength of others. Pardon us, for Jesus' sake.

In Your tender love for us You have given us Your only Son that in Him we may have eternal life with You. Pour out Your Spirit on us that we may have a strong and durable faith in Jesus' atoning work and at our end be brought into the fullness of joy in the presence of God, our Father. Amen.

Leader: Our Father, hear us as we offer our thanksgiving.

Elders: Praise to You, O God.

Leader: Jesus, Lamb of God, Savior of all, receive our worship.

Elders: Thanks be to You, O Lord.

Leader: Holy Spirit, Giver of life and salvation, Teacher and Guide, accept our exaltation.

Elders: To You be glory throughout the ages. Amen.

Make a Joyful Noise (Psalm 100)

1. Make a joyful noise to the Lord, all the lands!
2. Serve the Lord with gladness! Come into His presence with singing!
3. Know that the Lord is God! It is He that made us, and we are His; we are His people, and the sheep of His pasture.
4. Enter His gates with thanksgiving, and His courts with praise! Give thanks to Him, bless His name!
5. For the Lord is good; His steadfast love endures forever, and His faithfulness to all generations.

Alleluia! Let Praises Ring (Lutheran Worship, 437)

1. Alleluia! Let praises ring!
   To God the Father let us bring
   Our songs of adoration.
   To him through everlasting days
   Be worship, honor, pow'r, and praise,
   Whose hand sustains creation.
   Singing, Ringing: Holy, holy, God is holy;
   Spread the story Of our God, the Lord of glory.

2. Alleluia! Let praises ring!
   Unto the Lamb of God we sing.
   In whom we are elected.
   He bought his Church with his own blood,
   He cleansed her in that blessed flood,
   And as his bride selected.
   Holy, Holy Is our union And communion.
   His befriending Gives us joy and peace unending.

3. Alleluia! Let praises ring!
   Unto the Holy Ghost we sing
   For our regeneration.
   The saving faith in us he wrought
   And us unto the Bridegroom brought,
   Made us his chosen nation.
   Glory! Glory! Joy eternal, Bliss supernal;
   There is manna And an endless, glad hosanna.

4. Alleluia! Let praises ring!
   Unto our triune God we sing;
   Blest be his name forever!
   With angel hosts let us adore
   And sing his praises more and more
   For all his grace and favor!
   Singing, Ringing: Holy, holy, God is holy;
   Spread the story Of our God, the Lord of glory!

Te Deum in Unison (Lutheran Worship, p. 246—248)

You are God; we praise you.
You are the Lord; we acclaim you.
You are the eternal Father; all creation worships you.
To you all angels, all the powers of heaven, cherubim and seraphim,
    sing in endless praise:
Holy, holy, holy Lord, God of power and might, heaven and earth
    are full of your glory.
The glorious company of apostles praise you.
The noble fellowship of prophets praise you.
The white-robed army of martyrs praise you.
Throughout the world the holy church acclaims you:
Father, of majesty unbounded; your true and only Son, worthy of all
    worship; and the Holy Spirit, advocate and guide.
You, Christ, are the king of glory, the eternal Son of the Father.
When you became man to set us free, you did not spurn the
    virgin's womb.
You overcame the sting of death and opened the kingdom of heaven
    to all believers.
You are seated at God's right hand in glory.
We believe that you will come and be our judge.
Come, then, Lord, and help your people, bought with the price of
    your own blood, and bring us with your saints to glory
    everlasting.

Appendix E

Five Bible Studies for Elders Meetings

I Ephesians 5:15-20

Goal: That each elder identify and express thanksgiving as an exciting and essential element in his daily worship of God.

Our Concern

Share with one another your completed sentences:

1. I enjoy giving thanks to God today for this experience of this past week:
2. I struggle and find it hard to thank God for this experience of this past week:

St. Paul Speaks to Our Concern

1. Read aloud Ephesians 5:15-20.

2. Christians are called to be effective witnesses to people who do not yet know Jesus as their Savior. So Paul instructs Christians to conduct themselves wisely, not offending anyone, making good use of their time. "Wherefore accommodate yourselves to the time to such an extent that you even steal or rob the time as you may," Martin Luther wrote. He added, "Nothing ought to be more important to you than these efforts for the building of God's kingdom." No time is exactly right for Christian service because all days are evil. But be alert to your special opportunities. Take advantage of the time God gives you.

   Let Christ's Word dwell in you richly as you share with one another Biblical psalms, worship hymns composed by Christian poets, and the spiritual songs you frequently hear in Christian homes.

   Thanksgiving and praise are always the content of Christian hymns and other forms of worship. God's goodness and mercy in Christ Jesus generate such a response. Since God works all things together for our good, we have good reason to thank Him when tests, trials, and disappointments challenge us to rely on Him. We can also give thanks for all persons because God has poured out His mercy on everyone.

We Share Our Discoveries

1. Discuss the special steps Christians can take to guard against temptation and to make the most of the time (vv. 15-17).

2. Compare these two life-styles: (1) Drunk with wine; (2) Filled with the Spirit (v. 18).

3. Give examples of acts of worship which build you up in the faith (v. 19).

4. Suggest ways to show thanksgiving to God for the successes of the members of your zone or of the entire congregation (v. 20).

We Act on Our Decisions

1. To seize a special opportunity God has given me this week I _____
   _____

2. Today I _____
   in order by the power of God's Spirit to build up someone and to be built up myself in the faith of our Lord Jesus Christ.

3. Today with the Spirit and with words of thanksgiving to God I
   _____
   _____

II—1 John 4:13-21

Goal: That each elder compose a personal testimony of faith in which he confesses that Jesus is his Savior and the Savior of all people.

The Question: What does it mean for Christians to testify of, give a testimony about, or bear witness to Jesus, their Savior?

The Personal Reflection: Devote five minutes to quiet meditation. Turn over in your mind and heart your reluctance or eagerness to confess openly to others what Jesus means to you. Think deeply on abiding in God through faith in Jesus.

For Interpersonal Exchange: Discuss with an elder seated next to you some of your thoughts on the value of personal testimony or witness about Jesus to the people who hear it and the people who make it. Share some of your doubts or your excitement about your own past experiences.

For Group Discussion:
1. Read aloud 1 John 4:13-21.
2. How did what the early disciples of Jesus saw influence what they confessed?
3. How do Christians learn to love?
4. Describe the relationship between love and fear, fear and testimony, and testimony and love.
5. Give some examples of the tension between saying and doing love.
6. How does God's love establish the character and sustain the durability of our love and testimony?

To Summarize and Actualize:
1. Summarize in three sentences how the love of God kindles love in Christians.
2. The Father's love has sent His Son, Jesus, to be your Savior and the Savior of this world. In a brief paragraph compose your personal testimony to the power of that love.

III—2 Timothy 4:1-5

Goal: That each elder describe "sound Christian teaching" as he would like to experience it in parish events for learning God's Word.

Recall
Share with one another the memory of a person from whom you learned something valuable about being a Christian. Why was that person an effective teacher in that situation? How was your life changed?

Review
1. Read 2 Timothy 4:1-5 aloud.
2. How does the second coming of Jesus underscore the need to teach God's Word (v. 1)?
3. How do Christian pastors and elders "on duty and off duty" teach about Jesus (v. 2)?
4. When do people reject sound teaching and select teachers to suit their own likings (vv. 3-4)?
5. Give an example of a steady, disciplined, vigilant Christian teacher who turns away from novelties and myths and stresses the Gospel of Jesus Christ, the crucified and risen Lord and Savior (v. 5).

Rejoice

You are especially blessed by God through your membership in a Christian congregation which faithfully teaches and learns the Word of God. Thank God for your teaching/learning parish as it demonstrates the following:

Jesus is the Way, the Truth, and the Life.
The Holy Scriptures and the sacraments of Baptism and the Lord's
    Supper are God's means of grace.
The parish is a rich and creative context for growth in Christ.
The Word of God calls for commitment to God's purposes.
The methods of sharing God's Word depend altogether on God's full
    revelation of Himself in His Law and in His Gospel.
Christians are concerned for each whole person with whom
    they minister.

Renew

In His Word God instructs us by His law, calling us to repent, to confess our sin against Him; He invites us to turn away from every other hope and to put our confidence in Jesus. God also teaches us the joy of His salvation. By the power of His pardon He converts us to faith in Jesus and shapes our lives as His disciples. Every sound growth experience in a Christian congregation revolves around God's Law and Gospel, the message by which God calls us to repent and believe.

In your discussion with fellow elders commit yourself to sound Christian teaching. Discover what you would like to experience and help happen in the Bible classes and other teaching/learning events of your congregation.

IV—Mark 2:1-12

Goal: That each elder identify at least one person who is powerless because of illness, accident, poverty, or some other cause and propose at least one way to link that person with the power of God and the ministry of the congregation.

Write a Headline

1. Read Mark 2:1-12 silently.
2. Ask each elder to create for tomorrow's newspaper in your town a headline which announces the event recorded in Mark 2:1-12.
3. Discuss what you think the headlines would communicate to a modern reader.

Dig for Details

1. Who was the chief character in this event?

2. Who was powerless?
3. How did faith in Christ enable people to interact with and seek help for the powerless?
4. Why was Christ's word of absolution more difficult than His word of healing? How were the two related? How did Jesus respond to the whole person?
5. How did the man and those who observed the event react to the healing?

Report the Facts

Compose a paragraph for a modern newspaper account of the event. Include answers to the questions *who, what, where, why, when,* and *how.*

Editorialize

To editorialize is "to introduce opinion into the reporting of facts" or "to express an opinion in the form of an editorial."

Develop a brief editorial for your congregation's newsletter. Identify a person or a group of people in a situation of powerlessness similar to that of the paralytic whom Jesus healed. Suggest ways you and your congregation can expand your ministry as you try to link such people more closely with the power of God to forgive and heal.

V—Philippians 2:1-11

Goal: That each elder list at least one activity by which he and his congregation will improve participation or fellowship in God's Spirit.

Read

Open your Bible to Philippians 2:1-11 and take turns reading the verses aloud.

Mark

With a pencil, mark specific passages. ! [5] "I got it. I understand." ? [5] "I don't get it. I'm not sure what this means." < [5] "This lifts me up. I'm inspired." > [5] "I'm moving on. This leads me to new commitment." Discuss with another elder reasons why you marked the passages as you did.

Learn

1. How did the Philippian Christians give Paul joy (vv. 1-2)?
2. When do Christians appropriately look in on other people's interests (vv. 3-4)?
3. What kind of a mind do Christians have in Christ Jesus (vv. 5-8)?
4. Compare Jesus' state of humiliation with His state of exaltation (vv. 8-10).
5. How do modern Christians exalt Christ together (v. 11)?

Inwardly Digest
Paraphrase the two verses which speak most clearly to you and your situation. Think carefully about why you chose these verses.

Apply
Discuss with another elder something you want to work on in your relationship with other Christians in your congregation.

Suggest at least one activity in which you or a group of people can strengthen the spirit of fellowship in Christ in your parish.